FROM GIBRALTAR TO THE GANGES

Adapted from TO THE ENDS OF THE EARTH
by Irene M. Franck and David M. Brownstone

A Volume in the Trade and Travel Routes Series

Facts On File
New York • Oxford • Sydney

From Gibraltar to the Ganges

Facts On File, Inc.	Facts On File Limited	Facts On File Pty Ltd
460 Park Avenue South	Collins Street	Talavera & Khartoum Rds
New York NY 10016	Oxford OX4 1XJ	North Ryde NSW 2113
USA	United Kingdom	Australia

Library of Congress Cataloging-in-Publication Data

From Gibraltar to the Ganges: adapted from To the ends of the earth
  by Irene M. Franck and David M. Brownstone.
      p.   cm. — (Trade and travel routes series)
  Bibliography: p.
  Includes index.
    Summary: A historical survey of the Mediterranean-Black Sea
Routes, the Great Desert Route, the Persian Royal Road, and the
Indian Grand Road.
  ISBN 0-8160-1876-6
    1. Trade routes—Mediterranean Region—History—Juvenile
literature. 2. Trade routes—Middle East—History— Juvenile
literature. 3. Trade routes—India—History—Juvenile literature.
[1. Trade routes—History.] I. Franck, Irene M. To the ends of
the earth. II. Series.
 HE361.F745 1990
 382'.09—dc20   89-11693

British and Australian CIP data available on request from Facts On File.

Jacket design by Catherine Hyman
Composition by Facts On File, Inc.
Manufactured by R. R. Donnelley & Sons
Printed in the United States of America

10 9 8 7 6 5 4 3 2 1

This book is printed on acid-free paper.

CONTENTS

LIST OF MAPS

PREFACE

From Gibraltar to the Ganges is one volume in the *Trade and Travel Routes* series. The series is based on our earlier work, *To The Ends of the Earth*, published by Facts On File, Inc., in 1984. This adaptation of the work for young readers has been prepared by Facts On File; many new illustrations have also been added.

Several publishers gave permission to reprint selections from their works. In this volume, the excerpt on p. 98 is quoted from *The Travels of Fa-Hsien (391-414 A.D.) or Record of the Buddhist Kingdoms*, translated by H. A. Giles and published by Cambridge University Press in 1923. The exerpt on p. 13 is from the works of Herodotus, translated by A. D. Godley, published by Harvard University Press in the Loeb Classical Library in 1920, copyright © Harvard University Press. The excerpt on pp. 9-10 is from Homer's *Odyssey*, translated by E. V. Rieu, published by Penguin in 1946, copyright © the Estate of E. V. Rieu, 1946. The maps, drawn from *To the Ends of the Earth*, are by Dale Adams.

Irene M. Franck
David M. Brownstone

INTRODUCTION

What Is a Trade Route?

In a world without airplanes, engine-powered ships, trucks, or even paved roads, how did people journey from one place to another? How did products that were found only in a very small part of the world eventually find their way across the continents? For almost five thousand years, people have been bringing products from one part of the world to another using trade routes. Traders from Europe, Asia, and Africa carried furs, spices, silks, pottery, knives, stone utensils, jewels, and a host of other commodities, exchanging the products found in one area for the products found in another.

When trading first began, there were no real roads. Local traders might follow trails or cross steep mountain passes in their treks from one village to another. With the passage of time, tracks might be widened and eventually paved. But the new paved roads tended to follow the old trade routes, establishing these routes as important links of communication between different cultures.

As technology advanced, sea-lanes became vital trade routes between the various continents, and made possible trade with North America, South America, and Australia. Many of the highways and seaways that have been used predominantly for trade throughout history have shaped its course of events because of the many ways in which the routes have been used.

Why Study Trade Routes?

Studying the trade routes is one way of learning about the history of the world. As we look at the trade routes of Europe, for example, we can see how the nations of that continent have changed throughout the centuries: we learn how Scandinavian Vikings came to sail south and west to settle in France and Britain; we can appreciate how present-day Hungary was originally settled by a wandering tribe from the Ural Mountains, etc. In a similar way, by looking at the trade routes of Africa, we can trace the history of the slave trade and learn about the European colonization of Africa in the 18th and 19th centuries.

In addition, studying the trade routes helps us better understand the origin of many of the institutions and services with which we are familiar today. Postal systems, tolls, guidebooks, roadside restaurants and hotels all came into being, either directly or indirectly, because of trade routes. Studying the trade routes will help you to understand how they emerged.

How to Use This Book

This book is organized in chapters. Each chapter is devoted to the history of one trade route, or in some cases, where the particular trade route has an especially long and eventful past, to a particular era in a trade route's history. Therefore, you can simply read about one trade route that particularly interests you or, alternatively, read about all the trade routes in a given area. At the end of each chapter, you will find a list of books for further reading, which will assist you in locating additional sourcebooks should you need them to support report research or classroom work. If you are using these books as references for a particular history course, check the index of each to find the subject or person you need to know more about. The list of maps at the front of this book will direct you to all maps contained herein, and thereby help you to locate each trade route on the face of the earth.

Studying trade routes can be a fascinating way of learning about world history—and of understanding more about our lives today. We hope you enjoy all the volumes in the TRADE AND TRAVEL ROUTES series.

1

THE MEDITERRANEAN AND THE BLACK SEA ROUTES: ANCIENT PEOPLES

OUR SEA IN THE MIDDLE OF THE EARTH

The name of the Mediterranean Sea literally means the sea in the "middle of land." But many of the ancient peoples who lived around it simply called it "the sea," or "our sea." To them, it seemed as though all the countries in the world surrounded the Mediterranean.

In fact, the Mediterranean is at the center of three major regions—Europe, Africa, and the Middle East, and is connected to another sea, the Black Sea, which connects Europe and Asia.

The history of these two seas is the story of the various links between these continents—the trade and the travel that brought the great cultures of several peoples in contact with each other. The histories of Europeans, Africans, and Asians became intertwined as soon as people figured out how to sail and navigate the Black and Mediterranean seas to travel to other lands. The traders and travelers brought back new goods, new ideas, and new words to their home countries, and helped to shape the many great empires that grew up in this region.

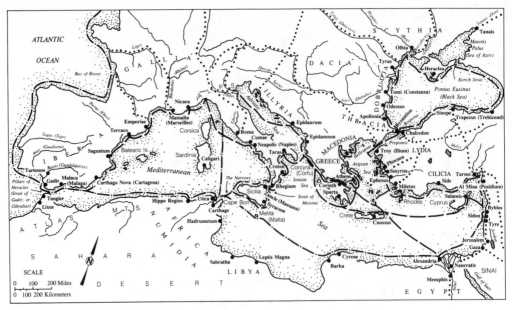

The Mediterranean and Black Sea Routes in Greek and Phoenician Times

—·—·— Main Phoenician Routes ·········· Main Connecting Routes
——— Main Greek Routes

Today these two seas are not so significant for trading purposes. The major trade and travel conducted in the world today makes use of other routes and other means of travel. Nevertheless, our culture—the way we think, the language we use, the ideas we have about the world—was very much shaped by the early peoples who visited each other across the Mediterranean and the Black seas.

THE SHAPE OF THE MEDITERRANEAN

Geology. The Mediterranean is a young sea. It was formed late in the history of the Earth, when the Atlantic Ocean broke through the narrow land bridge between Europe's Rock of Gibraltar and Africa's Rock of Ceuta. These two rocks now face each other across a narrow strip of water—known as the Straits of Gibraltar—rather than across a tiny strip of land.

When the Atlantic broke through this bridge, its salt water flowed into the Mediterranean, and through it, into the Black Sea. But fresh (unsalted) water from the rivers of Europe also flows into the sea. Because the fresh water is lighter, it forms a layer on top of the salt water. Because the bottom of the Mediterranean is very deep in some places but shallow in others, layers of fresh water and salt water form in different places. Thus the Mediterranean has many distinct areas, which differ a great deal.

Geography.   The Mediterranean Sea is divided like a butterfly into two halves, joined by a narrow "waist." In the middle—at the waist—is the island of Sicily. Between the northeast coast of Sicily and Italy lies the Strait of Messina. On its southwest coast, Sicily faces the 80-mile-wide passageway called The Narrows, which looks across to North Africa's Cape Bon, in Tunisia. According to the Bible, St. Paul was shipwrecked on the island of Malta, just east of The Narrows, in "a place where two seas met..."

   Beyond this narrow waist, the Mediterranean is a patchwork of many smaller seas: the Balearic, the Sardinian, the Ligurian, the Tyrrhenian, the Adriatic, the Ionian, and the Aegean. East of the Aegean Sea, waters flow into the mile-wide strait of the Dardanelles, also known as the Hellespont. This strait leads into the small Sea of Marmora, and on through the Bosporus Strait to the Black Sea.

Dangers of the Sea.   Of all the regions of the Mediterranean, the most dangerous is the African coast. This area is exposed to great gales, or sea storms, from the Atlantic Ocean, and there are few safe places to drop anchor. Other parts of the Mediterranean have their own dangers. North winds blow out of Europe between October and April, bringing storms to plague sailors. On the Black Sea, winter winds are sometimes so strong that they send up waterspouts. The early Greek poet Hesiod warned sailors to "avoid the winter sea when the winds war loud."

Sailing on the Mediterranean.   The Mediterranean is a summer sea, showing its kindest face to sailors from May through September. The Roman poet Horace suggested that "the sailing season begins in spring when the swallows build their mud nests under the eaves, when the meadows bloom, and the soft zephyrs blow over the unruffled sea." Of all the "unruffled seas" of the Mediterranean, the Aegean is the best for sailing, for it experiences the steadiest, surest winds. The modern writer Joseph Conrad called the Aegean Sea "that tideless basin freed from hidden shoals and treacherous currents." This is the sea where full-scale sailing on the Mediterranean seems to have developed.

The Early Sailors

Imagine how frightening—and how exciting—it must have been to explore the Mediterranean for the very first time. We do not know which people first sailed on the Mediterranean, or what kind of ships they used. But we do know that the Aegean Sea includes many islands that are quite close together. It must have been a marvelous discovery when early peoples realized that they could actually cross the water between the islands.

We do know that sailors arrived at Malta soon after 4000 B.C. And we imagine that the earliest vessels were not even boats, but probably dugout canoes (canoes "dug out" of logs) or rafts made of reeds tied together.

Eventually, of course, people began to build boats. At first, these were moved through the water by paddling. Paddlers sat in the boats facing the direction that they were going, pushing their paddles behind them into the water. Later, people discovered that it was faster and easier to row, sitting with their backs to the place they were going, pulling their oars instead of pushing them. Even after sails were discovered, people continued to row their boats as well.

With the development of sails, sea travel became much easier and faster. Sailing ships were developed in ancient Egypt, on the Nile River, and in the Middle Eastern countries around the Persian Gulf. The first sailing ships in the Mediterranean seem to have been used soon after 3000 B.C.

Trade and Cargo. Once sails were developed, it was possible to build bigger ships, ships that would have been too big to be powered by rowing alone. These bigger ships could carry cargo as well as people. Thus, *shipping*—carrying cargo by ship—was born.

There may have been shipping on the Mediterranean as soon as sailing ships appeared there, but the first written record of such activity dates from about 2650 B.C., during the reign of the Egyptian pharaoh (or king) Snefru. This written record consists of a note about bringing 40 ships of 100 cubits (about 12 to 18 feet) loaded with cedar wood from Byblos. Although this is the first written record, trade seems to have been well established by this time. The

Although Egypt traded with Palestine from very early times, Egyptians eventually withdrew from the Mediterranean and let others handle their sea trading. (By Manning de V. Lee, in Rupert Sargent Holland, *Historic Ships*, 1926)

cedar wood described was from the famous cedars of Lebanon, timber that the Egyptians used for thousands of years.

Tin and Amber. Despite their timber trade, the Egyptians were not long-distance traders. They usually traded only back and forth between Egypt and the coast of Syria and Palestine (modern-day Israel and Jordan).

Other peoples, however, did develop long-distance travel on the Mediterranean. Their motivation was trade. They wanted goods that they could only get from faraway places, so they had to develop trade routes to reach them.

The Bronze Age. One of the earliest materials that Mediterranean peoples wanted was tin. This was because tin could be mixed with copper to make *bronze*, a new metal harder than any that had been discovered up to that time. The *Bronze Age* was named for the discovery and early use of bronze.

Copper is the main metal in bronze, and there was a plentiful supply in the Mediterranean area, both in the Anatolian highlands (now part of the country of Turkey) and on the island of Cyprus. In fact, Cyprus got its name from the Greek word for copper. But tin, the other metal in bronze, was not plentiful in the Mediterranean area; there was some in Anatolia, but it was soon mined out. A new supply had to be found.

So, many hundreds of years B.C., early sailors set out of the eastern Mediterranean and up the Atlantic Ocean, as far as the British Isles and even beyond. Many of the greatest ports on the Mediterranean first became important because of their positions on the tin routes.

EARLY CULTURES

The earliest peoples of the Mediterranean lived in isolated villages, separated by land and sea from the other peoples of the region. As soon as they learned how to sail (and how to travel over land), however, they began to form larger communities and even empires that extended over land and sea. And peoples from small countries were able to reach out to others through trade and travel.

The Cycladic People. The earliest Mediterranean sailors to travel far outside the Egypt-Palestine area seem to have been voyagers from the Cycladic Islands. These islands are north of Crete in the Aegean Sea. By sailing along the northern Mediterranean coast for many weeks, the Cycladic people may have reached Iberia (modern-day Spain and Portugal) by 2500 B.C.

These early traders left no written records. However, archaeologists have found artifacts and remains from the same culture dating from this period at both ends of the Mediterranean.

The Minoans. The next great traders of the Mediterranean were the Minoans. They received their name from King Minos, their greatest ruler. The Minoans developed a great empire, whose capital was Cnossus, on the island of Crete. They were great traders, and seem to have traded from time to time with Cyprus, the Near East, and perhaps directly with Egypt.

Minoan trade began in 3000 B.C. By 2000 B.C., Minoan traders had set up a regular route around the southeastern Mediterranean. They had added the island of Rhodes to their trading route, and had extended their empire to rule some other islands nearby. Thousands of years later, in the ruins of their palaces, archaeologists found fine objects made of gems and precious metals that came from Egypt and the Near East, so we know that their rulers were prosperous.

The Minoans also sailed west in search of amber, a hard, jewel-like substance made of fossilized tree resin. Amber is gold or yellow in color and was often used in jewelry and other ornaments. The Minoans traded for amber with traders who had brought it from lands along the northern Baltic Sea.

Finally, the Minoans traded for tin. They themselves may have gone as far west as Spain, to meet with traders who had brought tin from Great Britain.

GREEKS AND TROJANS

The Greeks began to trade with the Minoans at around 1600 B.C., benefiting from their more advanced culture as well as their goods. These Greeks became sailors themselves, even taking some of the Egyptian and Syrian markets away from the Minoans.

Then, in 1500 B.C., the Greeks took control of Crete itself. They conquered the Minoans and fused both cultures together. The new culture came to be known as the Mycenaean culture, based around the city of Mycenae. The Minoan cities, including Cnossus, were destroyed—some by the Greek invaders, some by earthquakes. So control of the sea routes of the northern Mediterranean passed to the Mycenaean Greeks on the mainland.

The Mycenaeans Expand. The Mycenaeans took over the old Minoan trade and added to it their own trade with southern Italy. They also expanded trade with western Asia. Greek traders set up communities in many foreign cities. Then they went on to set up trading posts and pirate bases that actually became Greek *colonies*, lands outside of Greece itself that nevertheless were ruled and inhabited by Greeks. The earliest colonies were on the islands of Rhodes and Cyprus, and on the western and southern coasts of Asia Minor.

The Wealthy Trojans. These colonies brought the Mycenaeans into conflict with other peoples in Anatolia. One such people was the Hittites. Another was the Trojans, named for their city of Troy. (The city of Troy was also called *Ilium*. Today it is called Hissarlik.)

At that time, Troy controlled the Dardanelles (also called the Hellespont), the narrow strait that was the main crossing point from western Asia into Europe. Troy also commanded the water route from the Mediterranean into the Black Sea. Troy had other

The Dardanelles (Hellespont), in modern times defended by heavy cannon on one side and a fortified city on the other, long hindered early sailors. (From Montecuculli, *Commentarii Bellici*, 1788, MS. suppl. turc 226 f. 14v, Bibliothèque Nationale, Paris)

resources as well—the fertile farmlands around the city, and the copper mines of inner Anatolia. The Trojans prospered from these, and traded with the people of the northern Aegean Sea.

The Iliad *and the Trojan War.* One of the most famous poems ever written is called the *Iliad*: it is the story of a 10-year war between the Greeks and the Trojans (whose city was also called *Ilium*). We don't know how much of the story in the poem is true. But it is certainly true that the Greeks and the Trojans were rivals, for both wanted to control the trade routes in the eastern Mediterranean. After fighting for 10 years the Greeks were finally victorious and they burned the city of Troy to the ground—according to the *Iliad*.

The Odyssey. After the defeat of Troy, as described in the *Iliad*, Odysseus, one of the Greek leaders, sailed the Mediterranean back to his home city of Ithaca. His story is called the *Odyssey*, which describes many of the dangers of sailing on the Mediterranean. Even if the *Odyssey*'s stories do not ring true, they tell us what the dangers of the sea must have seemed like to these early sailors.

One portion of the *Odyssey* describes the perilous sail between Scylla, a huge sea monster perched on a rock, and Charybdis, a

From the city of Troy—behind the massive walls excavated in modern times—the Trojans controlled the sea routes through the Hellespont (Dardanelles), in the background. (From James Henry Breasted, *Ancient Times: A History of the Early World...*, 1914)

whirlpool that sucked ships into its depths. Ships had to pass between these two dangers. It seemed almost certain that a ship that avoided the deadly whirlpool would be attacked by the huge monster.

Odysseus was a skilled sailor. He had been told that the lesser of these two evils was Scylla. The monster might kill some of his sailors—the whirlpool would certainly kill all of them. So he sailed cautiously into the narrow straits, as the *Odyssey* describes it:

> Thus we sailed up the straits, groaning in terror, for on the one side we had Scylla, while on the other the mysterious Charybdis sucked down the salt sea water in her dreadful way. When she vomited it up, she was stirred to her depths and seethed over like a cauldron on a blazing fire; and the spray she flung on high rained down on the tops of the crags at either side. But when she swallowed the salt water down, the rocks re-echoed to her fearful roar, and the dark sands of the sea bottom came into view.
>
> My men turned pale with fear; and now, while all eyes were fixed on Charybdis and the quarter from which we looked for disaster, Scylla snatched out of my boat six ablest hands I had on board. I swung round, to glance at the ship and run my eye over the crew, just in time to see the arms and legs of her victims dangled high in the air above my head. "Odysseus!" they called out to me in their agony. But it was the last time they used my name....Scylla had whisked my

comrades up and swept them struggling to the rocks, where she devoured them at her own door, shrieking and stretching out their hands to me in their last desperate throes. In all I have gone through as I made my way across the seas, I have never had to witness a more pitiable sight than that.

The *Odyssey* tells us that Odysseus made it through the dangerous straits, losing no more than six of his men to the monster Scylla.

Does this story have any basis in fact? Scholars think that perhaps Scylla signifies the dangers of the sea, such as the rocks and stormy waters that took the lives of many early sailors. Charybdis may represent the whirlpools of the Strait of Messina, between Italy and Sicily. There the waters of the eastern and the western halves of the Mediterranean meet. This meeting of the waters forms deadly currents and eddies that are dangerous even today. In ancient times, the Mediterranean's seabed was in a different position, and so these straits were even more dangerous. Perhaps the *Odyssey* was describing them.

Doric and Ionian Greeks. If there really was a Trojan war, Troy was probably destroyed by the Greeks sometime between 2000 and 1300 B.C. But it is also possible that both Troy and the Greeks were attacked by a new wave of invaders, the Dorians, who also came down from the north.

For many years, historians believed that these Dorian Greeks attacked all the cities of Greece, and that only Athens survived. Refugees from all the other cities went to Athens. Although today we are not sure whether this theory is true, we do know that many of the original Greeks fled to the region of Attica, where Athens is located.

These refugees drove yet another group of Greeks, the Ionians, out from the mainland into the Greek islands and across to the western coast of Asia Minor. Mycenae and its culture were destroyed. The culture survived in the colonies that had been founded, but the Mediterranean trade routes collapsed.

The End of an Era. With the invasion of the Dorian Greeks came the end of an era. The Bronze Age was superseded in the eastern Mediterranean by the Iron Age. Iron had long been used in the Near East and in Africa. But the Dorian Greeks were the first to bring iron weapons into Greece. From now on, this would be the principal metal used by the most advanced peoples of the world.

THE PHOENICIANS

Other invaders also came into the eastern Mediterranean. One of the most important was the Phoenicians. Phoenicia was not a single nation. It was a confederation of city-states—cities that operated like little independent countries. When the Greek trading routes collapsed, the Phoenicians were ready to take them over. From their home port of Byblos, they moved out into the Mediterranean Sea in force.

The Phoenicians were good sailors. They used strong, well-crafted boats, made from the cedars of Lebanon. Their chief ports were the cities of Sidon and Tyre.

For three centuries, between 1200 and 900 B.C., these Phoenicians were the masters of the Mediterranean. They brought raw materials from the western Mediterranean, especially wheat, oil, wine, and tin. These they traded to the more developed cultures of the eastern Mediterranean, along with their own products—timber, purple dye, and expertly made glassware.

Phoenician Colonies. At first, the Phoenicians concentrated on the eastern Mediterranean. In the 11th century B.C., they set up their own colonies on Cyprus and Rhodes, and used these bases to trade with peoples in Asia Minor and in the Aegean Sea. Then they headed west across the more open seas of the Mediterranean. They were headed for Iberia (modern-day Spain and Portugal), which was rich in tin.

The Phoenicians not only braved the open waters of the Mediterranean, but also sailed at night, for they were able to sail by the stars. They especially made use of the North Star to guide them. When the Greeks later learned this skill from the Phoenicians, they called the North Star "the Phoenician Star."

In 1200 B.C., the Phoenicians are said to have founded a city on the Atlantic coast of Iberia. They called it Gadir; its modern name is Cadiz. Perhaps the Phoenicians did not found this city, but only discovered it. In any case, it became one of their main ports and their entryway to the mines of Iberia.

The Phoenicians also founded colonies on the North African coast. Utica, at the Narrows, was founded around 1100 B.C. Over the next

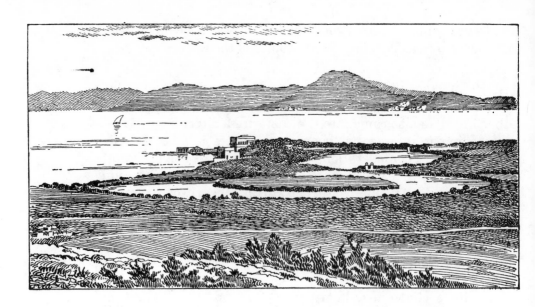

The harbor of Carthage, shown here in an early 20th-century view, provided much-needed protection for ships on the low-lying North African coast. (From James Henry Breasted, *Ancient Times: A History of the Early World...*, 1914)

few centuries, they founded Tangier on the Strait of Gadir (now the Strait of Gibraltar), and Malaca (now Malaga) in southern Spain. Phoenicians set up colonies in Sardinia, Malta, western Sicily, and the Balearic Islands as well, so that they eventually controlled all the key points on their route through the southern Mediterranean, from Tyre to Gadir. In 814 B.C., the Phoenicians founded a new city, known as Carthage. Today, Carthage is near the city of Tunis, in the North African country of Tunisia. Carthage became a very important Mediterranean trading center.

The Phoenicians were clearly the main sailors of the age. They may even have sailed around Africa, from east to west, in order to arrive at Gadir.

Trade and Barter. Like the other early peoples, Phoenicians did most of their trading by *barter*. That is, rather than taking money for goods, they simply exchanged them for other goods. That's because, in those early days, there was no one currency that could be used in all different countries. So rather than selling goods and buying other goods with the money, people preferred to barter.

When these ancient peoples did not know each other's languages, they had to barter silently. Can you imagine how you would trade with someone if you did not speak the same language? The fifth-century Greek historian Herodotus describes how the Phoenicians went about their trade on the Atlantic coast of what is now Morocco. By this time, the city of Carthage had become the new center of the

Phoenician empire, and the Phoenicians therefore became known as the *Carthaginians*:

> Another story too is told by the…[Carthaginians]. There is a place in Libya, they say, where men dwell beyond the Pillars of Hercules [Strait of Gadir, or Gibraltar]; to this day they come and unload their cargo; then having laid it orderly along the beach they go aboard their ships and light a smoking fire. The people of the country see the smoke, and coming to the sea they day down gold to pay for the cargo and withdraw away from the wares. Then the…[Carthaginians] disembark and examine the gold; if it seems to them a fair price for their cargo, they take it and go their way; but if not, they go aboard again and wait, and the people come back and add more gold till the shipmen are satisfied. Herein neither party (it is said) defrauds the other; the [Carthaginians] do not lay hands on the gold till it matches the value of their cargo, nor do the people touch the cargo till the shipmen have taken the gold.

Certainly the two people must have trusted each other very much for this kind of trade to work!

Elsewhere, the Phoenicians were not trusted. In the Greek poems the *Iliad* and the *Odyssey*, Phoenicians are accused of kidnapping women and children, and making them work as slaves.

However, these stories may not be true. By the eighth century B.C., the Greeks were beginning to revive their trade. Naturally, they had to compete with the powerful Phoenicians. Perhaps they told these stories in order to make their rivals look bad.

During this period, the Phoenicians did withdraw from the Aegean Sea, leaving trade in that area to the Greeks. But they kept control of all of the routes along the southern Mediterranean.

MEDITERRANEAN PIRATES

When trade became more regular and more prosperous, traders became the targets for thieves and pirates. The Greeks might have accused the Phoenicians of stealing—but they themselves had pirates waiting in ambush in the mouths of rivers or on the far side of peninsulas. The pirates hid in light boats or rafts, which were easy to keep out of sight, then swarmed toward ships that came too close. Other pirates acted as wreckers, using false signals to lure ships onto rocks, where they crashed or were captured.

Not only the Greeks practiced piracy. Many other peoples did, too. Some peoples carried it on in large groups, so that it sometimes became very similar to warfare. Other poor people used it as a regular way of making a living, for there was no other on some rocky coasts. The fifth-century Greek historian Thucydides describes piracy as a normal activity:

[Some people] turned to piracy…with a view both to their own gain, and to maintenance for the needy, and falling upon towns that were unfortified…they rifled them, and made most of their livelihood by this means; as this employment did not yet involve any disgrace, but rather brought with it somewhat of glory.

This vase painting, redrawn by a modern artist, shows a Greek sea fight in about 700 B.C. (From James Henry Breasted, *Ancient Times: A History of the Early World…*, 1914)

Strong states were sometimes able to control piracy somewhat. But pirates would continue to be a danger throughout the history of the Mediterranean, even into the 20th century. That's why many early people set their cities high on rocky points, far from the shore. They also had a complex system of beacon (or signal) fires and flares, to warn of the approach of strange ships.

Neither the Greeks nor the Phoenicians were united as citizens of a single country. Although both the Greek race and the Phoenician race spoke a similar language within each race and shared a common culture, each Greek or Phoenician people was more loyal to the city-state they came from than to a country called "Greece" or "Phoenicia."

The Greeks were known as *Hellenes*, after *Hellas*. Hellas was originally a town in Thessaly, in the north, but eventually the name came to be applied to the whole region. Hellas is still the Greek word for the country of Greece today. Nevertheless, the ancient Hellenes were more loyal to Athens, Sparta, some Greek colony in Asia Minor, or one of the other Greek city-states than they were to "Hellas" in general. Each of the city-states had its own area of control and influence.

The Black Sea Region. The Black Sea region was generally controlled by the city-state of Miletus, near the southwest corner of Asia Minor. The people of Miletus took their woollen goods east to trade for grain (mostly wheat), metals, wood, fish, and slaves. While doing so, they became the first Greeks to fully explore the Black Sea and to found major towns along its shores.

In early galleys like this one, the Greeks explored all the way from the Black Sea to the Pillars of Hercules (Strait of Gibraltar). (By Manning de V. Lee, in Rupert Sargent Holland, *Historic Ships*, 1926)

In the middle of the seventh century B.C., Greek colonists founded the city of Byzantion, on the north side of the Bosporus strait. This city would much later be known as Byzantium, the principal city of the Eastern Roman Empire, and, many years after that, the capital of the empire of the Ottoman Turks. Today the city is known as Istanbul and is located in modern Turkey.

The Western Daughter States. The western Mediterranean also saw Greek expansion and settlement. Citizens of Corinth went west to take control of the island of Corfu and later conquered part of Illyria (modern Albania). The Corinthians might have gone farther, but they were stopped by fierce pirates, as well as by strong winter winds. (Even today, some towns in the northern Adriatic region provide guide ropes on their main streets, which people must cling to when the winds blow hard.)

Southern Italy and Sicily were also colonized by the Greeks and these areas came to be known collectively as Magna Graecia. These lands were fertile and rich in grain, as well as covered by many forests.

The western colonies were used as stepping stones by the Greeks to sail farther west, to Spain. The greatest Greek sailors were the Phocaeans, who lived on the mid-western coast of Asia Minor. The Phocaeans settled Massalia, present-day Marseilles, France, which was quite close to Spain. Soon after their arrival in 600 B.C., they began to challenge the Phoenicians as long-distance traders.

The Phoenicians took up the challenge. They blockaded the Strait of Gibraltar for most of two centuries, between the late sixth and the fourth centuries B.C. Even so, Phoecaean Greeks occasionally managed to slip through.

Still, for most of this period, the Phoenicians controlled Iberia, so the Phocaean Greeks had to be satisfied with trading overland. These Greeks founded many trading colonies in areas that today are in France, including Nicaea, known today as Nice, and Heracles Monacus, today the principality of Monaco.

The Decline of the Phoenicians. As the Greeks were expanding throughout the Mediterranean, the Phoenicians were losing strength. The people of Phoenicia itself eventually lost their independence, and their western colonies became more important to them. Gradually, the Phoenicians became known as Carthaginians, after their western city of Carthage (near today's Tunis, in Tunisia).

Eventually, Carthage controlled the southwestern Mediterranean, including almost all contacts with the Atlantic.

THE PERSIAN WARS

By 513 B.C., the Persians had taken control of Phoenicia along with the rest of western Asia. The Persians are the ancestors of the modern Iranians. They were excellent soldiers and found a clever way to cross the Hellespont—on a bridge of boats. Once they crossed, they conquered the region between Macedonia (part of today's Yugoslavia) and the Black Sea.

Twenty years later, in 493 B.C., the Persians fought the Greeks in the Aegean Sea. Their fleet was mainly made up of Phoenicians, who were all too happy to have a chance to fight the Greeks. The Persians and the Phoenicians won—and went on to burn and plunder many Greek cities in Asia Minor and on the Aegean islands.

There were several more major battles between the Persians and the Greeks, including the famous battles of Marathon and Thermopylae. Eventually in 479 B.C. the Greeks were successful in finally defeating the Persians.

THE PELOPONNESIAN WARS

Once the Greeks had stopped the threat from Persia, they began to fight amongst themselves. Eventually, two shifting groups of alliances appeared—Athens and its Delian League, and Sparta and its Spartan Confederacy. In 431 B.C., these groups began the Peloponnesian Wars, which continued for decades. The wars got their name from the Peloponnese, the great southern peninsula of Greece.

Ironically, the fifth century B.C. was the heyday of classical Greece. This was the period in which Greeks developed the art, philosophy, science, and political theory that was to shape thought and culture in Europe for centuries to come, right through our own day. Greek ideas on drama were formed by, among others, the fifth-century playwright Euripedes, whose plays are still performed today. Greek philosophy grew to great prominence in this period, and was strongly influenced in particular by Socrates. Likewise, the great ruler Pericles and the important historian Herodotus lived in fifth-century Greece.

Yet the fifth century B.C. in Greece was a time of almost continual fighting, either with foreign powers, or with other Greek states.

Finally, Greece would be united. But this unity brought new changes, for it was created by an outsider, Philip of Macedon, who conquered Greece in 338 B.C. Philip's son was Alexander the Great, the man who built a huge empire that included Greece and its old enemy, Persia. Alexander heralded the beginning of a new era in the Mediterranean and the Black Sea lands—the age of empire.

2

THE MEDITERRANEAN AND THE BLACK SEA ROUTES: THE EARLY EMPIRES

NEW EMPIRES OF THE MEDITERRANEAN

Alexander the Great was a Macedonian leader who in the fourth century B.C. conquered many lands around the Mediterranean. At its height, his empire included parts of Greece, Persia, Phoenicia, and Egypt.

Alexander's empire heralded the dawning of a new era. For the first time, huge empires would control vast territories around the Mediterranean and would reach beyond the Mediterranean to conquer or influence peoples of Africa and the East.

Some empires rose to power and were supreme in the region for several centuries. Some empires lost power quickly, or shared it with others. The story of these empires is the story of their efforts to expand and maintain their power, often in competition with other powers.

ALEXANDER THE GREAT: THE FIRST MEDITERRANEAN EMPIRE

Alexander was the son of Philip of Macedon, who had conquered Greece. (Today, the ancient region of Macedon [Macedonia] is split in three between Greece, Bulgaria, and Yugoslavia.) In 334 B.C., Alexander went on to fight a series of battles in the Near East, breaking the power of the Persians.

Alexander's mighty armies seemed unstoppable. They met serious resistance only when they reached the island city of Tyre. Today, Tyre is a city in Lebanon, but in Alexander's day, it was part of the old Phoenician empire. Alexander fought to gain control of Tyre throughout most of the year of 332 B.C.; eventually he was victorious. In order to defeat the citizens of Tyre, Alexander had built a causeway, or bridge, from the mainland out to the island. The remains of his causeway still exist today. Alexander could make use of the causeway to attack from both the land and the sea. This victory over Tyre marked the end of the great empire of Phoenicia. From then on, the Phoenicians were known as Carthaginians, since the city of Carthage became their new center.

Alexander's City. Alexander went on from Tyre, south and west across the Gaza Strip into Egypt. There he founded a new port on one of the western arms of the Nile. It would be named Alexandria, after him. This city still exists today, and is part of Egypt. Alexander continued to push eastward after gaining control of Egypt, but none of his subsequent successes could match his achievements in Egypt. When he died his empire was divided among his lieutenants.

ALEXANDRIA

Alexander had an enormous impact on world events. The peoples of the Mediterranean were now looking beyond their shores toward the great markets of the East. Alexander had reached out by land to the great markets of the East—China, Japan, and the Spice Islands, where silks, jewels, and precious spices were traded. His heirs also reached out by sea to Arabia and India.

Precious Goods of the East. Egypt and the Near East had been trading with the Far East for a long time. But it was not until after Alexander had built his empire that Egypt began to trade extensively with other peoples around the Mediterranean Sea.

In those days, spices were grown only in the Far East. Cinnamon, pepper, and other such seasonings grew in the lands that today are the countries of Malaysia and Indonesia, among other Far Eastern nations. The Chinese made the world's best porcelain, and the

Chinese, Japanese, and Indians wove wonderful fabrics of silk and cotton. All these goods were extremely valuable to the people in the Mediterranean area.

Today, these goods are readily available. It is easy to fly them around the world, or to ship them on huge cargo ships. It is also possible to manufacture porcelain and textiles in many different parts of the world. But in those days, if you wanted spices, silks, and other luxury items, they had to be attained from the Far East.

Thus, it was a significant change for the peoples of the Mediterranean when they began to receive these goods through trade with Egypt. Many of these goods were shipped through the new port of Alexandria, a trading center for the Greek-controlled part of the Mediterranean world.

Alexandria's Wonderful Lighthouse. Alexandria had a great lighthouse on Pharos Island. It was over 400 feet high and its light—fire reflected and magnified by mirrors—shone many miles out to sea. The lighthouse made it easier for sailors to steer their ships into port. Alexandria was also a great cultural center. It drew on the best of three continents—Europe, Africa, and Asia. Scholars and scientists from throughout the Greek world went to Alexandria to conduct research, study, and teach. This Egyptian city soon replaced cities on mainland Greece and Asia Minor as the center of learning and culture for the region.

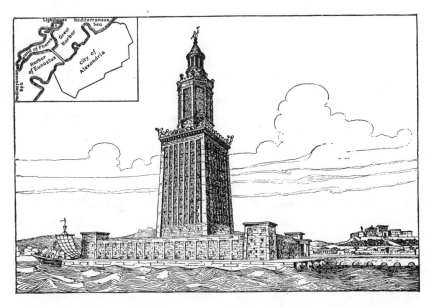

The great lighthouse on the island of Pharos was one of the Seven Wonders of the World; the inset shows the location of Pharos in relation to the city of Alexandria. (From James Henry Breasted, *Ancient Times: A History of the Early World...*, 1914)

Alexandria was the cultural center of the eastern Mediterranean. But in the western Mediterranean, a new power was being born— Rome.

By the third century B.C. Rome was strong enough to challenge the powerful city of Carthage. The Romans wanted to take control of the important Messina Strait away from Carthage. Naturally, Carthage resisted. The result was the great series of conflicts known as the Punic Wars. These wars were named by the Romans from the Carthaginians' old name for "Phoenicians," rendered *Poeni* in Latin.

New Battle Tactics. The Romans suffered early losses. Roman soldiers were far more effective than the Carthaginians, but they had no experience of the sea. The Carthaginians, of course, had been great sailors for many years. However, the Romans were quick to learn. According to legend the Romans captured a Carthaginian ship and had their own shipbuilders copy it to make their own fleet. But the Romans did not simply copy—they also improved.

The main battle tactic employed in naval warfare on the Mediterranean up to this point had been to ram the enemy ship with a hard, pointed prow, trying to sink the ship by making a big hole in it. The Romans came up with a new idea. They used a gangplank—a long plank of wood that went from the deck of one ship to the deck of another. The clever Romans lowered their gangplanks onto the enemy's ship and stuck it into the deck with a spike called a *corvus*. The spike made a hole in the deck, and made it difficult for the enemy to throw the gangplank overboard. Once the gangplank was in place, Roman soldiers could easily cross it to board the enemy's ship. Then they were no longer engaged in a sea battle. Instead, they were fighting hand to hand—and that was what the Romans excelled at.

By the end of the First Punic War in 241 B.C., Rome had expanded much of its Mediterranean territory. Besides controlling Sicily, it also controlled the islands of Sardinia and Corsica, and thus the vital Tyrrhenian Sea. The Carthaginians, once a Mediterranean power, retreated to North Africa.

This victory also provided the Romans with a base from which to conquer the western Greeks. From then on, Greek culture would be an important influence on Roman thought, politics, and art.

The Carthaginians Expand. With their loss of control in the central Mediterranean, the Carthaginians looked to the west. They had always traded with Spain, and even beyond. Now they actually founded colonies in those lands. One such colony they called New Carthage, "Carthago Nova," which is now the Spanish city of Cartagena.

The Second Punic War. Since the First Punic War, although the Carthaginians were still active traders, they were no longer a great sea power. The Second Punic War broke out in 218 B.C., when the Carthaginian leader Hannibal invaded Italy, in an effort to regain Carthage's former power. But this time, battles were fought almost entirely on land. Hannibal's invasion is especially famous for the elephants that he brought with him from northern Africa. To enter Italy overland, Hannibal had to take a route that took him through the mountain range called the Alps. The elephants were needed as baggage animals, to bear the supplies and weapons of the Carthaginian soldiers.

Hannibal and his army were victorious against the Romans in a number of battles, and for a while it looked as though they might crush the Romans. However, the tide turned, and Hannibal was forced to return to Africa. There, in 202 B.C., the decisive battle of Zama was fought, which was an enormous defeat for the Carthaginians. The battle of Zama was effectively the end of the Second Punic War.

The Third Punic War. Even after this second defeat, Carthage still hung on. It traded with nations bordering the Atlantic and expanded its holdings in northern Africa. But in 149 B.C., the Romans moved to finish off the remains of the once-great empire. Claiming that the Carthaginians had broken the treaty formed in 201 B.C., they attacked Carthage itself.

The Romans laid siege to Carthage—that is, they surrounded the city and would not let anyone bring food or supplies into the besieged area. At first the Carthaginians were well protected from the Romans by a triple wall, but in the end, they were starved out.

The Romans wanted to make sure that Carthage would never again pose a threat to them. They burned the city to the ground. The site smouldered for days. When it had finally cooled, the Romans sprinkled salt on it, so that nothing could ever be grown there. The people of the city were killed or sold into slavery.

The Punic civilization had effectively been wiped out by the Romans. Though, during the long wars the Romans had probably learned as much from the Carthaginians as they had from the Greeks about sailing, trading, and farming.

ROME MOVES EAST

After the Punic Wars, Rome turned its attention to the eastern Mediterranean. Both the Greeks and the Syrians had allied themselves with Carthage against Rome. So the same year that they razed (tore down) Carthage, the Romans conquered the Greek city of Corinth. Soon afterwards, they conquered Athens, too.

Invading soldiers here plunder Corinth, a city grown rich because of its location on a short overland shortcut between the Aegean and Adriatic seas. (From L. W. Yaggy and T. L. Haines, *Museum of Antiquity*, 1882)

Then Rome moved through northern Africa, traveling east from Carthage toward the Red Sea. They also moved farther into Asia Minor, and to the Black Sea. The whole area around the Aegean Sea had become a battlefield as the Romans tried to take control of it. Here is the description of a Roman traveler writing in 45 B.C.:

As I was returning from Asia, I looked at the coastlines about me. The island of Aegina lay astern [behind], and Megara before me. On my right was Piraeus [the port city of Athens], and on my left was

Corinth. These were all once prosperous, highly populated cities—but now they lay before my eyes ruined and devastated.

So as it established its own empire, Rome devastated both Carthage and Greece.

ROMAN TRADE AND TRAVEL

Before the Roman Empire, the Mediterranean had been crisscrossed by a number of different routes. As the Romans rose to power, that all changed. They were the first, and the only, rulers ever to unite the whole Mediterranean area. As part of this process, they changed the area's focus: on land and on sea, all roads and routes led to the city of Rome.

However, the Romans still were not sailors. Although they had huge ships for trade and travel, they relied on others to build and sail them. The Greeks, the Carthaginians, and the other good sailors among the conquered peoples were the backbone of the Roman navy.

Rome itself was called "a city without a harbor," for it was not actually on the sea. In order to sail into Rome, ships had to pass through 15 miles of the muddy Tiber River. In the early days, ships brought grain and other goods from Egypt to nearby ports. The goods were then brought overland to Rome.

In addition to the great grain fleets of Rome, smaller merchant ships sailed the Mediterranean, serving local needs. (Vatican, Rome)

Rome depended on grain from Egypt, Spain, and the Black Sea to feed its huge population. Besides these necessities, Rome was also a very rich market for luxuries, mainly from the Far East. From Egypt, Rome sent Greek sailors to develop direct trade with India and the rest of the East. That way, Rome did not have to depend on the Arab traders who had been middlemen, going between Europe and the East. Eastern goods also traveled overland, from China through Central Asia, into Syria.

THE LAST DAYS OF THE ROMAN REPUBLIC

During the middle of the first century B.C., Rome was beset by civil war, as opposing politicians competed to gain control of the Roman army and of Rome itself. Two of these figures were Julius Caesar and Pompey. During these times of uncertainty, the Mediterranean shipping routes were constantly disrupted by attacks from pirates. The grain ships that traveled from Egypt were threatened, putting Rome's food supply at risk. Thus Pompey was given the mission of clearing the Mediterranean of pirates. He destroyed hundreds of ships, captured hundreds more, and killed or resettled thousands of pirates. All this obviously made Pompey a very popular figure.

The rivalry increased between Pompey and Caesar until they finally went to war against each other. Caesar was eventually victorious and became absolute dictator of Rome for life. This marked a major change in the Roman system of government, which up until then had been a republic with elected officials. Other politicians were disturbed by Caesar's new powers and combined to kill him in 45 B.C. Caesar's nephew, Octavius, was Caesar's successor, and after more bloody civil wars, he finally became the first emperor of Rome in 31 B.C. He adopted the new name of Caesar Augustus on becoming emperor. The heyday of the Roman Empire was about to begin.

THE DAYS OF ROMAN RULE

With Caesar Augustus came the era known as the *pax Romana*, or "Roman peace." The name comes from the relative peace that held throughout the Mediterranean for 200 years, a peace that depended on the Romans maintaining their position of power, so that any challengers could be quickly put down.

The Roman peace was maintained by a fleet of ships spread throughout the Mediterranean. There were ships on the Gallic Coast, on Italy's Bay of Naples, at the city of Ravenna on Italy's Adriatic coast, at the island of Malta, and at many other places in the eastern Mediterranean. Troops from these places could be shipped at short notice to wherever they might be needed. If a revolt did start, these troops could be used to put it down. Sometimes they were also used to expand Roman borders.

THE DECLINE OF ROME

By the third century A.D., the Roman Empire began to weaken. For centuries, Rome had derived its strength from conquering new peoples and incorporating them into the empire. Then peoples from the north began sweeping down, invading the Roman Empire and refusing to become part of it.

The Empire Moves East. In the fourth century A.D., the emperor Constantine decided to build a "New Rome" in the eastern half of the empire. He chose the old Greek town of Byzantion, which the Romans called Byzantium. Later, the town was renamed again. In honor of the emperor, it was called Constantinople. (Today it is the city of Istanbul, in modern Turkey.)

The founding of Constantinople was the beginning of an important shift in the Roman Empire. Up to that point, the center of the empire was, of course, Rome itself. But after Constantinople was founded, the center of the empire began to shift eastward.

Invaders and Pirates. The western Mediterranean continued to be invaded by various northern peoples. In the fifth century, Germanic invaders swept into Italy and even sacked Rome itself. By this time, no Roman fleet was left in the western Mediterranean, and the government, fearing the invaders, had actually left Rome! They ran away to Ravenna, a coastal city of canals whose houses were built on stilts to keep them high above the watery ground.

Without the Roman fleet to patrol the waters, pirates came back to the western Mediterranean. Trade and travel were disrupted by both pirates and invaders. One group of invaders, the Vandals, took an unwary merchant fleet in 425 A.D. and swept across to North Africa. They conquered most of the territory immediately, with only a few walled cities holding out. One city that held out, ironically, was Carthage—which the Romans had rebuilt 100 years after they had torn it down.

In 429 A.D., however, even Carthage came into the pirates' hands. The Vandals saw that Carthage was strategically located to enable them to control east-west sea-lanes, and they made this ancient city their capital. They also conquered Sicily, Sardinia, and Corsica. This cut off the Italian mainland from the sea, and helped force the final collapse of the Western Roman Empire. The Eastern Roman Empire still flourished, however. Its capital was at Constantinople. It became known as the Byzantine Empire.

The Vandals were not traders, but plunderers. For at least a century after their invasion, piracy was the rule in the western Mediterranean, and in much of the eastern as well. The only peaceful places were the Aegean and the Black Sea, where the Byzantine Empire's fleet still prevailed.

The Moslems

In the seventh century, a new religion was founded: the religion of Islam, whose followers are called Moslems. Islam was founded in Mecca, which is part of the modern country of Saudi Arabia. Over the centuries, it spread throughout the Middle East and eastward to parts of India. Like Judaism and Christianity, it remains an important world religion whose history continues to influence millions of people.

The Moslems Expand. The Moslems were not at first a seagoing people, but they soon became one. They drew on the Greek learning they found in Syria and in Alexandria. They also drew on Syrian and Egyptian contacts with the rich trade to the Far East.

Like the Romans, the Moslem Arabs used native sailors from the ports of Egypt, Palestine (the modern-day countries of Jordan and Israel), and Syria to control the southeastern Mediterranean. They captured the islands of Cyprus and Crete. Then they raided the Aegean and attacked Byzantine ships that sailed west past Greece. The Byzantines responded by cutting back their seagoing trade. Instead, they shipped goods over land.

Attack on Constantinople. However, the Byzantines could not avoid all Moslem attacks. Constantinople itself was attacked several times in the seventh century. In the eighth century, it suffered a full-scale siege.

Constantinople was a well-protected city. It was surrounded by heavy walls. Beyond that lay not land, but sea, for the city was located on a peninsula, overlooking a great harbor known as the Golden Horn. The entrance to the harbor was protected by a heavy chain strung across its entrance.

The people of Constantinople also had a secret weapon: Greek fire. This was a liquid that could catch fire. It was invented by the Greeks, but was refined in the seventh century. The burning liquid was shot out from behind the city walls to set fire to approaching ships. Greek fire could also be launched from ships. Many centuries later, an Italian captain described how the Byzantine ships

> ...had at their prow the head of a lion or other land animal, made of brass or iron, with the mouth open, and all gilded so that the very aspect was terrifying. The fire which he directed against the enemy was passed through tubes set in the mouths of these beasts, so that it seemed as if the lions and other monsters were vomiting fire.

Greek fire was called "Greek" because Constantinople was very influenced by Greek culture. At this time, with the Western Roman Empire in ruins, Constantinople was the center of both Greek culture and of Christianity. Although it had once been the center of the Eastern *Roman* Empire, its main language was Greek.

Early Greeks used "liquid fire" to repel invaders, as the later Byzantines do here against Vikings from northern Russia. (Bibliothèque Nationale, Paris)

Arab Expansion in the West. The Byzantines stopped Arab expansion in the east. But nothing could stop them moving west. They swept across North Africa, conquering lands and converting people to Islam. Finally, they took the Strait of Gibraltar, the gateway between the Mediterranean and the Atlantic Ocean. The Strait of Gibraltar is bordered on its north and south sides by two rocks. The rock on the African side is known as Ceuta. The European rock is called Gibraltar. This name originally came from the Arab name, Jebel-al-Tariq, which means "Rock of Tariq." If you pronounce the Arab name aloud, you can hear where the sound "Gibraltar" came from.

The Arts of the East. Throughout the Mediterranean, the Arabs spread the arts and the crafts of the East. Because they traveled back and forth between Europe and the Far East, they were an important link between East and West, bearing both goods and knowledge.

The peoples of the East had made some major advances in navigation that were to be quite helpful to those in the West. For example, the Chinese had invented the magnetic compass, in which a metal needle is magnetized, so that it always points north. This was useful in figuring out directions when sailors were so far out at sea that they could not be guided by landmarks. They had also discovered a better way of calculating latitude; that is, of measuring where a ship was in relation to all the landmarks around it. In addition the Arabs pioneered the use of the triangular *lateen* sail, which made it possible to sail against the wind. Centuries later, Europeans would use this Arab and Eastern contribution to build huge ships that sailed far out into the ocean to explore the Western Hemisphere.

However, most of the Arab sailing was done along the Spice Route, the routes that led them to the Far East, where they could trade for spices and other precious goods. The Arabs did not do much trading on the Mediterranean, where they were as much pirates as traders.

Conflicts Between Arabs and Christians. The main conflict to emerge in the Mediterranean was between the Moslem Arabs and the Christian Byzantines. The Byzantines managed to beat back Arab raids into the Black Sea. But the Arabs took Crete in 823, which boxed Byzantium in. Crete was used as an Arab pirate base for raids into the Aegean. It was also a slave market where captives were sold.

In the ninth century, the Arabs also took most of Sicily. Some fortified cities, especially Syracuse, resisted for many years, but essentially, the area belonged to the Arabs.

The Arabs went even farther west, moving into Spain and Portugal. From there, they attacked almost every major port in the west, including Marseilles and Nice (in modern France), and Genoa and Ostia (in modern Italy).

The conflict continued. But in the 10th century, the Byzantine Empire revived somewhat. The Byzantines took back Crete, and for a time, some parts of Sicily.

The Rus—Ancestors of the Russians.   The Arabs, however, were essentially the masters of the Mediterranean at this time. Therefore, the Byzantines depended more on trade in the Black Sea area. There they traded with a new people—Vikings, or pirates, from Sweden, known as the Rus. These were the ancestors of today's Russian people. The Rus ran the only active trade route across Europe during the ninth and 10 centuries. Another trading partner on the Black Sea were the Jewish Khazars, who lived in the mountains of the Caucasus. They traded on the Black Sea at the port of Tana, on the Don River.

MOSLEMS AND CHRISTIANS

The rivalry between Moslems and Christians continued into the 10th century. Both groups wanted to control the Mediterranean; each group had its own areas of influence. Eventually, however, Arabs and Christians settled down to an uneasy truce. They traded with each other mostly in peace, though pirates still threatened the seas.

The Seljuk Turks.   The relative peace between the Moslems and the Christians continued into the 11th century. That was broken by the appearance of two new rival groups. One major group was the Seljuk Turks. Originally from Central Asia, this people expanded, conquering Syria and Palestine. Soon they annexed most of Asia Minor.

For many years, Christians had made religious journeys, or *pilgrimages*, to Jerusalem, in Palestine. But the Seljuk Turks decided that they did not want Christians crossing their lands. They

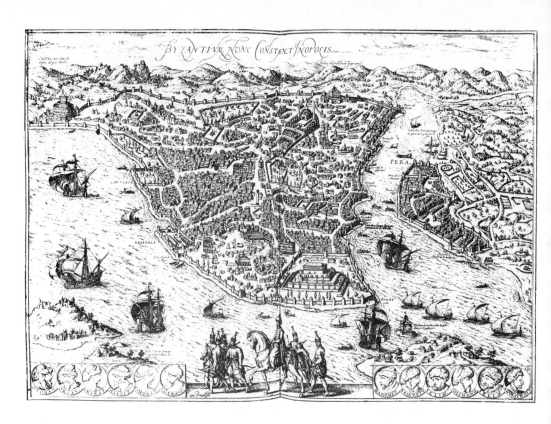

In its days of greatness, Constantinople was a crossroads of the world, and its port was much admired among Mediterranean sailors. (From G. Braun and F. Hogenberg, *Civitates Orbis Terrarum*, Cologne, 1576)

cut the pilgrimage routes, refusing to allow Christians to cross through Moslem territory.

The Seljuk Turks also presented a serious threat to the city of Constantinople, which at that time was still a Christian city, the center of the Eastern Orthodox Church. Constantinople appealed to the West for help.

Normans. A second group threatened the Byzantines at the same time as the Seljuk Turks—the Normans. The Normans were a branch of the old Norwegian Vikings, or Norsemen. Many centuries before, they had settled in northern France. In the 11th century, they went south, seizing the area of southern Italy from the Byzantine Empire. They gained control of the Strait of Messina and, defeating the Moslems, made themselves masters of Sicily and Malta, in the process dominating Mediterranean east-west sealanes. The Normans were now set on controlling the rest of the Byzantine Empire. They disguised their plan by pretending to want to win lands from the Moslems for Christianity. The Crusades provided the Normans with an excuse.

Hoping to come to the aid of the Byzantine Empire threatened by the Seljuk Turks, in 1095 at a Church council meeting at Clermont, France, Pope Urban II called on Christians to take back the Holy Lands from the Moslems.

The Crusades (the name comes from the cross on the uniforms of the Christian soldiers) were the so-called "holy wars" that Christians fought in an effort to gain control of huge sections of the Middle East at the expense of the Moslems who had cut their pilgrimage routes.

Ships from Europe's Mediterranean coast transported pilgrims, merchants, and Crusaders—as well as horses like those being unloaded here. (National Maritime Museum, Greenwich)

People joined the Crusades for different reasons. Some were genuinely religious and were outraged at the Moslems' actions. Others were seeking adventure, the excitement of travel to foreign lands. Still others, like the Normans, saw the Crusades as the chance to make their fortunes, to win rich lands or capture important segments of the East-West trade. At this time, Arabs were still the main carriers of Far Eastern goods to the West. Europeans prized the silks, spices, and jewels that Arabs brought, and may have hoped to take part in this activity themselves.

The Crusades lasted for over 200 years. There were many temporary changes in land ownership. For a time, the Christians did regain control of parts of the Middle East. But in the end, the Moslems prevailed. However, many Christians did make their fortunes in the Crusades, and East-West trade did expand as a result of Europe's increased contact with the rest of Asia.

The Italian City-States. Among those to benefit from the Crusades were the Italian city-states of Genoa, Pisa, and Venice. Early in the Crusades, Christian Crusaders had gained control of the ports of Syria and Palestine. That meant that traders, pilgrims, and Crusaders could take sea routes from Europe to the Middle East. The Italian ports were well placed to take advantage of this new traffic. Over the centuries, these city-states sent knights and pilgrims off to the East. They also received Eastern goods and Eastern culture. Gradually, the Italian city-states became rich and powerful. Both their riches and their new culture set the stage for the later Renaissance, or "rebirth"—the flowering of science, ex-

Venice, city of islands, became rich transporting pilgrims and Crusaders to the Holy Land. (From G. Braun and F. Hogenberg, *Civitates Orbis Terrarum*, Cologne, 1576)

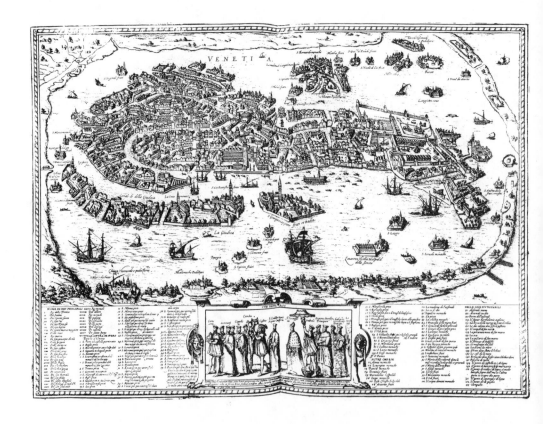

ploration, literature, and art that eventually spread through Europe in the 15th century.

Genoa and Venice. Genoa and Venice soon came to control the Mediterranean routes—Genoa in the west and Venice in the east. Both reached for the more distant markets of the Black Sea. Sailors from these cities soon replaced Greek traders from Constantinople, even in the Aegean and the Black Seas.

Constantinople. Constantinople was still considered a great city, but mainly as a meeting place for other travelers. The Jewish 12th-century traveler Rabbi Benjamin ben Jonah described the city's diversity like this:

> All sorts of merchants come here from the land of Babylon [modern-day Iraq]…from Persia [modern Iran], Media, and all the sovereignty of the land of Egypt, from the land at Canaan [modern-day Lebanon] and the empire of Russia, from Hungaria, Pazinakia [modern Rumania], Khozaria [the kingdom of the Khazars, in the Caucasus Mountains], and the land of Lombardy [one of the regions of Italy,

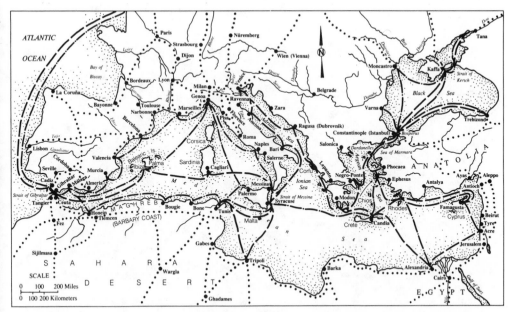

The Mediterranean and Black Sea Routes in Medieval Times

—·—·— Main Genoan Routes   ·········· Main Connecting Routes
— — — Main Venetian Routes

then its own kingdom] and Sepharad [Spain]. It is a busy city, and merchants come to it from every country by sea or land, and there is none like it in the world except Baghdad, the great city of Islam.

But in spite of this activity, Constantinople was declining. By the 13th century, the Greek historian Nicetas wrote that the Byzantine admiral "had sold the anchors, sails, and everything else belonging to the Byzantine navy that could possibly be turned into money." The city's defensive walls—the walls that were supposed to protect it against attack or siege—had also fallen into disrepair.

Constantinople became vulnerable to attack, and eventually Venice took control of the city. Even though the Crusaders generally attacked the Moslems, on this occasion Venice pushed the knights of the Fourth Crusade to attack their fellow Christians, the people of Constantinople. The once-great city was *sacked*; that is, it was looted and robbed. The knights and their Venetian partners split the loot among themselves. In fact, St. Mark's Church in Venice is still decorated by some beautiful bronze horses that were actually stolen from Constantinople.

The Byzantine Empire still survived in a weakened form. It was to hang on for another two and a half centuries, sometimes under an Italian ruler, sometimes under a Greek ruler. But the leaders

With ships like these, Christian knights carried on running sea battles with their Moslem opponents. (By Manning de V. Lee, in Rupert Sargent Holland, *Historic Ships*, 1926)

were now controlled by either Venice or Genoa. The empire's great days were over.

The Moslems Expand. Meanwhile, the Moslems in the eastern Mediterranean were reviving in the late 12th century, under the Egyptian leader Saladin. During the 13th century, the Moslems gradually drove the Christians out of all the lands they had taken in the Middle East.

A powerful magnet for would-be conquerors for centuries, Constantinople (now Istanbul) looks across the Bosporus from Europe (in the foreground) to Asia. (From James Henry Breasted, *Ancient Times: A History of the Early World...*, 1914)

Some knights then went back to northern Europe. But others stayed in the Mediterranean. The best known of those who stayed on are the Knights Hospitallers of St. John. The Knights was a religious and military group devoted to protecting pilgrims in the Holy Land. Its members were both soldiers and caretakers. After the Moslems took back the Holy Land, the Knights of St. John went to Cyprus, which was then the main meeting place for Christian and Moslem traders. There, Moslems passed their much-prized Far Eastern goods on to Christian traders, who carried them back to Europe.

Knights of St. John captured the island of Rhodes from the Moslems and from there they protected Christian shipping routes in the eastern Mediterranean and raided the coasts of Moslem-held lands.

The Knights had light, fast galleys which they kept ready during the summer months, when the Mediterranean was calmest. On Rhodes itself, the Hospitallers built heavy defenses. The 15th-century Jewish traveler Obadiah da Bertinoro, describing the island fortress, wrote, "No one who has not seen Rhodes, with its high and strong walls, its firm gates and battlements, has ever seen a fortress."

When the last Christian stronghold fell to the Moslems in 1291, the Crusader era virtually ended. But the Crusades left their mark on Europe. The new infusion of Eastern learning led Western scientists to begin new explorations in their own scientific tradition. And the new and valuable trade with the East inspired kings and princes to search for new trade routes to India, Africa, and China. The money from the increased trade helped pay for these trips as well as provide strong incentive for them: the new era of exploration and cultural rebirth known as the Renaissance was about to begin.

3

THE MEDITERRANEAN AND THE BLACK SEA ROUTES: FROM THE RENAISSANCE TO MODERN TIMES

THE MEDITERRANEAN: SEA OF THREE CONTINENTS

From the earliest days of human history, the Mediterranean Sea routes were a way for isolated peoples to connect with one another. Gradually, over the centuries, the region began to be tied together through trade and travel. Africans, Asians, and Europeans were connected by the sea that lay between them.

These connections grew during the Renaissance and the period just before it. The word "renaissance" means "rebirth." It is given to the period of the 15th century in Europe because during this time, Europeans experienced a "rebirth" of interest in expanding the limits of knowledge, culture, and exploration. Scientists began performing new experiments in physics, astronomy, and medicine. Artists rediscovered ancient Greek techniques of depicting human anatomy. And explorers began to sail south toward Africa and east toward Asia, in an effort to expand trade.

During the 15th and 16th centuries, the goods of the Far East were still among the finest in the world—and they could not be gotten anywhere else. China, India, Japan, Malaysia, Indonesia, and other eastern lands produced fine silks, cottons, tableware, ornaments, jewels, and, above all, spices. Until then Europeans had depended on Arab traders to bring these products from the East. At that time, Europeans did not even know the shape of Africa, and had not acquired the knowledge that could enable them to sail east themselves.

Then various European countries began to sponsor voyages of exploration, in an attempt to capture this profitable trade for themselves by finding a sea route to the East, since Moslems had closed overland routes to them. This began a period of expansion. First the Europeans expanded their trade and travel to the East. Then, over the centuries, they took control of huge portions of India, Indonesia, and Egypt, ruling these countries as colonies. Naturally, this led to competition between the Europeans themselves, as well as fighting with the peoples they had come to dominate.

The story of the Mediterranean from the Renaissance to the present is the story of this expansion and the competition that resulted.

VENETIAN TRADERS

Venice Expands. From the mid-14th century on, the Italian city of Venice had grown ever stronger in the Mediterranean. Venice was ideally situated to trade with the Arabs who brought goods from the East. The money—and the Islamic culture—that they brought to Venice helped the city grow rich and powerful.

Venice soon took control of the main islands of the Mediterranean, including Crete. But the city was more interested in trade than in religion or war. After the Moslems regained control of the Middle East and expelled Christians from their land (see Chapter 2), Venice quickly made trade agreements with the Arabs, and began to trade actively with the Near East and Egypt.

War with Genoa. Another Italian city, Genoa, also wanted to control the Mediterranean. The two cities fought a naval battle just north of Sicily, in 1373, which Venice won. Genoese ships still sailed the Mediterranean, but Venice was the most powerful city.

Venice's success was all the more remarkable because of the dangers of the Adriatic Sea. The late 15th-century Jewish traveler Rabbi Meshulla Ben R. Menahem described the passage to Venice like this:

> ...[the Adriatic Sea] is very dangerous because of the numerous rocks, and there are also places where the sea is very shallow, and anyone not acquainted with the place can come to grief with his ship or his vessel by grounding or striking the rocks...

The north winds blasting out of Europe made the Adriatic coast around Venice even more difficult to navigate. Rabbi Menaham describes his passage north in October 1481:

> ...we were in a canal...and some of the sailors wished to hoist the big sail and other sailors said that this is not the time to hoist because the wind is strengthening; and there was a dispute between them, and finally they decided to hoist the sail, but they could not, and [it] was torn...the mast was almost shifted, and all the sailors and we and all the pilgrims [religious travelers to and from the Middle East] took hold of the mast but were not able to keep it upright, and we were in very great danger....
>
> On the same day, at night, there was thunder and lightning and heavy clouds on the mountains, and rain pouring on the ground with a deafening east wind like I have never seen in my life, and a sea came upon us when we were near the sail and we were nearly stranded....I swear that I heard the sailors say that never since they had been at sea had they seen so powerful and evil a wind as that, for the waves passed over all sides and every corner of the ship, and it went under water and then came out; but God saved us from that tempest....

Spain and Portugal. Venice did not dominate the Mediterranean for long. Spain and Portugal also wanted a part of the rich trade in spices and silks. They did not have the experience that the Italian cities had—so they hired Italian sailors to navigate their ships! Ironically, Genoa, which was losing the competition with Venice, had lots of unemployed sailors—so these same sailors helped two other countries win the trading competition against Venice.

Portugal, in particular, began a series of explorations, using expert Italian sailors. By the end of the 15th century, this tiny country had found the Cape of Good Hope route, which circles all around the continent of Africa and then continues eastward to China and India. With the help of Venice's Italian rivals, the Portuguese cut Venice out of the spice trade almost completely during the 16th century.

Spain also employed Genoese sailors. The most famous of these may have been Christopher Columbus, who sailed west in hope of arriving in the East. Columbus didn't know that there were two continents in his way—North and South America. Spain continued to explore the Americas and began an active trade across the Atlantic.

With the opening of the Cape route to Africa and the Atlantic routes to America, Europeans had little interest in the Mediterranean after the 16th century. Sometimes they even called it "the Forsaken Ocean."

THE TURKS

The Ottoman Empire.   Asians, however, were still interested in this central ocean. In 1453 the Ottoman Turks, newly converted Moslems, conquered the Christian city of Constantinople and made Islam the official religion. Constantinople became the capital of the new Ottoman Empire.

The Turks were happy to have a base on the Black Sea, and quickly moved down to the Mediterranean. They soon became a great sea power. They cleared away the pirates who had come to inhabit the Mediterranean, and took control of many of Venice's island bases. They even forced Venice to pay them an annual tribute, or tax, for the privilege of trading in the region.

It was the Turks who gave the Black Sea its modern name. And they began to call the city of Constantinople by a new name, which, centuries later, became official—Istanbul.

The Barbary Pirates.   In the 16th century, a new group of pirates came to settle in the Mediterranean. These pirates came from many places. One group had come into being as a result of the Turks' expansion. By the early 16th century, the Ottoman Empire had taken control of Greece. Then it moved over the sea to the ancient city of Carthage, which by then had been given the new name of Tunis (its modern name, in modern-day Tunisia). Some raiding

Turks became pirates on the Barbary Coast between Tunis and the Rock of Ceuta (the rock facing Gibraltar).

At the same time, the Spanish were expelling at least 300,000 Moriscos. These were Spanish Moslems who had accepted Christian baptism, but whose conversion was not sufficient to please the Catholic authorities of the time.

As a result, Moriscos eager for revenge also became pirates on the Barbary Coast. So did other Christian and Jewish outcasts. Eventually, the Turkish, Christian, and Jewish pirates went beyond the Strait of Gibraltar to attack the great Spanish galleons (large ships) that brought gold and silver from America.

The pirates seized many rich goods that Spain and other nations were bringing back from around the world: gold, silver, amber, spices, pearls, and silks. They brought these back to their home bases, among them the city of Algiers (in the modern-day country of Algeria, in North Africa), captured by the most famous of the Barbary pirates, a Turk named Khizr. The Moslems knew him as Kheir-ed-Din, or "Protector of the Faith." The Christians called him Barbarossa—"Red Beard."

The Turks did not do much about the Barbary pirates, who were often their allies. But they did do something about the Christian Knights of St. John Hospitalers—the religious and military order that attacked Turkish ports and vessels. In 1522 they expelled the Knights from their stronghold on Rhodes. The Spanish helped the Hospitalers settle on the island of Malta. Later, the Knights became so identified with their new island home that they became known as the Knights of Malta.

In 1521 the Ottoman Turks drove the Knights of St. John Hospitalers from their fortress at Rhodes to the sanctuary of Malta. (From *Sulayman-nama*, 1557, H. 1517 f. 149r, Top-kapi Saray Library, Istanbul)

CONFLICT ON THE MEDITERRANEAN

Galley Slaves. Conflicts between Turkish Moslems and European Christians continued. One result of their battles was a source of sailors. In the past, ships were run by free sailors. Even if a people had been conquered by another people, the subject people who chose to be sailors did so freely. If there was war, the subject sailors would share in the fighting. If there was loot, they would share in the spoils.

But during the 16th century, when there were so many Moslem and Christian skirmishes, both sides began to use their captives as

These Christian fathers have arrived in one of the pirate ports along the Barbary Coast, to ransom enslaved Christians like those at the right. (Engraving by P. Dan, British Library Board)

slaves to row their huge ships. These ships were known as galleys, so the slaves were known as galley slaves. It was during this period that sailing ships developed. It had become possible to sail huge ships long distances, relying mainly on wind to cross the ocean. But oared ships had to be used on the Mediterranean, for there, the winds were not dependable.

Thus Turks used their Christian prisoners of war to row their galleys. And Christians used their Turkish slaves as rowers. (Later, Christians would also force criminals and people in debt to row, as well.) Malta thus became a major slave market, with the Knights of St. John Hospitalers selling the Turks they had captured during their raids.

The life of a galley slave was so hard that even today we use the expression "to work like a galley slave" when we want to describe endless, back-breaking labor. Much later, a French naval officer, Barras de la Penne, described the life of these slaves:

Many of the galley-slaves had no room to sleep at full length, for they put seven men on one bench; that is to say, on a space about ten feet long by four broad....The creaking of the blocks and cordage, the loud cries of the sailors, the horrible maledictions [cursing] of the galley-slaves, and the groaning of the timbers are mingled with the clank of chain. Calm itself has its inconveniences [because of] the evil smells which arise from the galley.

Fighting in the Mediterranean. To help fight their Christian enemies, the Turks called the pirate leader Barbarossa out from Algiers to become admiral of the Turkish fleet. He succeeded in ousting Venice from its last possessions in the Aegean Sea.

Venetians, Genoese, and Spanish joined forces to fight the Turks, but their naval forces were very weak. Earlier sea battles were fought using the old Roman technique: ram into a ship, board it, and continue the fight by hand. The Turks had developed a new, more effective fighting technique, however—the broadside. They simply shot cannon balls straight across the water at the enemy ships.

Although the Europeans lost the first battles, they eventually beat the Turks in 1571 at the Battle of Lepanto. This battle also established another major change in naval combat. In the old days of ramming and boarding, oared galleys had been a useful type of ship. The men who rowed could maneuver the ship during the fighting,

After the Battle of Lepanto, oared Turkish ships, like those shown attacking the Venetian flagship, were largely abandoned for sailing ships. (By Manning de V. Lee, in Rupert Sargent Holland, *Historic Ships*, 1926)

and might even be able to fight themselves. With the broadside, however, it was better to have sailing ships, which could more easily keep their distance and escape the cannons. These ships were armored with metals or hardwood, as protection against both the cannon and the wood-eating *teredo* worm.

The Northern Europeans

The British Expand. As European explorations opened up the East and the Americas, more and more northern Europeans used the Mediterranean as a shortcut to these other lands. The English, the Dutch, and the Scandinavians sailed to the Mediterranean to trade, and as a jumping-off point for travel farther east. The British, for example, sent couriers through the Mediterranean to India. Eventually, the British claimed huge sections of India and ruled that nation as a colony. The British also claimed the Rock of Gibraltar. And they set up a base at Naples, so that they controlled the north-south route in the central Mediterranean.

Scurvy. The northern Europeans built huge ships that could sail out into the open waters of the sea. Navigation techniques had advanced so that they no longer needed to hug the coast, as earlier ships did. Some of the British ships were able to go for as long as four months before putting into port.

But these long journeys created new problems. The food that could be carried without spoiling on a four-month journey was missing some important vitamins and minerals. The lack of vitamin C produced a disease called scurvy. It took a long time to cure the disease, for no one knew what caused it. Finally, however, it was discovered that giving sailors lemons from Sicily kept scurvy away. We now know that lemons contain vitamin C! Later, British sailors were given limes. That's how "limey" became a slang word for a British sailor.

British-French Conflict. Gradually the British and the other Europeans made peace with the Barbary pirates. The pirates began accepting tribute, or payment, as a kind of pay-off for not attacking European ships. Later, the Knights of St. John Hospitalers surrendered Malta to the French, under Napoleon, on his way to taking the Egyptian city of Alexandria.

Conflicts with the pirates might be over, but conflicts among the Europeans had just begun. The French expansion into Alexandria did not please the British. These two powerful nations became enemies who fought throughout the Mediterranean. Fighting between the two nations continued throughout the era of Napoleon Bonaparte, a corporal in the French army who rose to power and eventually crowned himself emperor of the French.

Napoleon was a great military leader and managed to conquer many of the independent states of Europe, including those of Italy. However, his military might proved to be no match for the British. In 1815, he fought his final battle, near the city of Waterloo, in Belgium. There he was defeated by a combined British and Prussian (from Prussia, a German state) force.

British Expansion. After the victory at Waterloo, the British were able to claim territory taken by France in Egypt, as well as gain firm control of Gibraltar and Malta. The British were expanding quickly in the East, especially in Egypt and India.

The Mediterranean was important to the British, for it offered a shortcut to the East. British soldiers, traders, messengers, and adventurers could sail through Gibraltar and across the Mediterranean, from where they could then take overland routes from the Near East or Egypt to the Indian Ocean.

British naval power was supreme in the world at this time, and this also helped the British to expand. In 1827, a British, French and Russian fleet had smashed a Turkish fleet, breaking Turkey's hold on the routes into the Black Sea. That also led to independence for Greece, formerly part of the Ottoman Empire. Britain and France took possession of land that Turkey had once taken from Venice and Russia gained control of the mouth of the Danube River.

Britain's strength in the Mediterranean made for many changes: English became the common language among Mediterranean traders; British officials and British tourists began to appear regularly in the eastern Mediterranean; and the British introduced modern machines into the Mediterranean, especially the steamship. This type of transportation was ideal for this sea, for it was not affected by lack of wind.

The Crimean War. Meanwhile, Turkey continued to weaken in the eastern Mediterranean. Its weakness offered an opening to other powers. Disputes in the 1860s among Turkey, the Western Europeans, and the Russians led to the Crimean War. This conflict between Russia and the allied powers of Turkey, Britain, France, and Sardinia ended in Russia's defeat, increasing British power and stopping Russia's expansion in the area. The Russians were forced to open up the Black Sea to ships of all nations, leading to further British and European expansion into the region.

The Suez Canal. Another long-term change in the Near East was brought about by the construction of the Suez Canal (built between 1859 and 1869). This canal linked the Mediterranean and the Red Sea, making East-West travel and trade far easier than ever before.

There were now coaling stations for steamships at Gibraltar, Malta, and Port Said in Egypt. The Mediterranean revived, for it was now the main sea route in the world, connecting Europe to the Far East via the Red Sea. It was no longer an enclosed inland sea, but the midsection of a seaway spanning one-quarter of the globe.

MODERN TIMES

World War I. The early 20th century saw a conflict that was to change the map of Europe. The First World War was chiefly a European conflict involving most of the Western powers. Britain, France, Russia, and later Italy and the United States joined forces against Germany, Austria-Hungary, and the Ottoman Empire. These nations all had colonies or spheres of influence throughout the Mediterranean, the Middle East, and Africa. Their competition for trade, as well as for colonies, had finally intensified into a major war.

Most of World War I's battles were fought on land and the British bases at Gibraltar, Malta, and Alexandria, guarding the sea routes that brought armies to many strategic areas, were decisive factors in the defeat of the Ottoman Empire and the conquest of Germany's overseas colonies.

World War II. The period just after World War I was a difficult time. Many countries were impoverished because of the huge costs of the war and experienced social unrest. But European countries still wanted to maintain and expand their colonies.

In Italy, a new leader, Benito Mussolini, was promising to make his country as great as it was in the days of the Roman Empire. His was a brutal dictatorship based on fascism, a system of government that emphasizes strict control over the people of a country and conquest of other peoples considered to be weaker. Mussolini reached across the Mediterranean into Africa, trying to conquer Ethiopia.

Meanwhile, in Germany, Adolf Hitler was also building a fascist government. He, too, wanted to glorify his country at the expense of others.

In Asia, Japan expanded into Manchuria and China. Eventually, Italy, Germany, and Japan formed the Axis. They fought the Allies—Britain, France, the Soviet Union, and the United States—when war broke out.

During this war, a worldwide conflict drawing in nearly every country in the globe, the Mediterranean was one of the main battlefields. Italy took control of Rhodes and Germany took control of Crete. The British held onto Gibraltar, Malta, and Egypt. The Allies therefore controlled the main East-West routes, and threatened the north-south supply routes between Italy and North Africa.

Malta provided the key to the Allies' eventual victory. In November, 1940, a new type of ship—the aircraft carrier—was based at Malta. These ships made possible a crippling air attack on Italy's southern base at Taranto.

Malta was severely bombed by German and Italian air forces and at times could be supplied only by submarines. Even so, Allied forces there were able to disrupt Axis supply lines, especially the flow of oil, which the Axis needed to drive its tanks and support its land armies. Malta was also the base for the Allies' successful invasion of Sicily, a key part in the Allies' eventual victory.

Long after Venice's great days as a world power, it remains famous as a uniquely beautiful city, shot through with canals. (By A. H. Hallam Murray, in *Sketches on the Old Road Through France to Florence*, 1904)

After the War: The Suez Canal Incident. When World War II ended, Middle Eastern oil became very important to the economies of the world's industrial countries. Thus, attention became focused on the Suez Canal since it was an important means of transporting that oil from the Middle East to Europe via the Mediterranean.

The British gradually lost their empire in the Far East as India and other countries pressed for independence. The lands around the Mediterranean likewise fought to break free from the British Empire and its influence. In 1956, Egypt decided to nationalize the Suez Canal—that is, to declare that it belonged to Egypt, rather than to the British. The British resisted this decision, but in the end, Egypt prevailed.

In 1967, Egyptian control of the Suez Canal became important in a new way. Egypt decided not to allow Israeli ships to use the canal. This decision led to a war, which closed the canal for several years.

Eventually, the Suez Canal reopened. But by that time, oil tankers generally followed the much longer route around the Cape of Good Hope and newer giant oil tankers were too large to be able to use the Suez Canal.

The Mediterranean Today. In the late 20th century, the great passenger liners that had once passed through the sea on their way east gradually lost ground to airlines. But the Mediterranean today is still a magnet for tourists and travelers from around the world. Travelers sometimes fly to the region and then sail around it on cruise ships. Sailing ships are no longer used for serious travel, but they are used for recreation. Today, however, sailing craft are equipped with motors, for the uncertain winds of the Mediterranean can still fail a craft that relies on sails alone to propel it.

SUGGESTIONS FOR FURTHER READING

Bradford, Ernle. *Mediterranean: Portrait of a Sea* (New York: Harcourt, Brace, Jovanovich, 1971).

Casson, Lionel. *The Ancient Mariners: Seafarers and Sea Fighters of the Mediterranean in Ancient Times* (New York: Macmillan, 1959).

Connolly, Peter. *Greece and Rome at War* (Englewood Cliffs, New Jersey: Prentice-Hall, 1981).

Cornell, Tim, and John Matthews. *Atlas of the Roman World* (New York: Facts On File, 1982).

Grant, Michael. *The Ancient Mediterranean* (London: Weidenfeld and Nicolson, 1969).

Harden, Donald. *The Phoenicians* (New York: Praeger, 1962).

Hoskins, Halford Lancaster. *British Routes to India* (New York: Octagon Books, 1966), reprint of the 1928 Longmans Green edition.

Hyde, Walter Woodburn. *Ancient Greek Mariners* (New York: Oxford University Press, 1947).

Levi, Peter. *Atlas of the Greek World* (New York: Facts On File, 1980).

Ludwig, Emil. *The Mediterranean: Saga of a Sea* (New York: Whittlesey House, McGraw-Hill, 1941), translated from the German by Barrows Mussey.

Morand, Paul. *The Road to India* (London: Hodder and Stoughton, 1937).

Ormerod, Henry A. *Piracy in the Ancient World: An Essay in Mediterranean History* (Totowa, New Jersey: Rowman and Littlefield, 1978), reprint of the 1924 work.

Semple, Ellen Churchill. *The Geography of the Mediterranean Region: Its Relation to Ancient History* (New York: Holt, 1931).

Tavernier, Bruno. *Great Maritime Routes: An Illustrated History* (London: Macdonald, 1972), translated from the French.

4

THE
GREAT DESERT ROUTE
AND THE
PERSIAN ROYAL ROAD

THE ROADS THAT WENT THROUGH EMPIRES

The story of the Great Desert Route and the Persian Royal Road is the story of the development of some of the world's great empires. Forming an empire meant conquering many peoples and much land. The empire would last as long as it could keep its subjects under control and fight back against other peoples. When a new group proved stronger, the old empire would fall and a new one would take over.

At first these empires were formed by people living in the Middle East, in the desert regions through which the roads ran. Later, these empires were ruled by Europeans. Finally, many countries and peoples fought for their independence. Their battles helped shape the map of the Middle East as it is today.

However, for all of these empires and these nations, the Great Desert Route and the Persian Royal Road were important. These roads were used by rulers to send soldiers wherever they were needed, to conquer new lands or control old ones. The roads also allowed people at one end of an empire to communicate with those at the other.

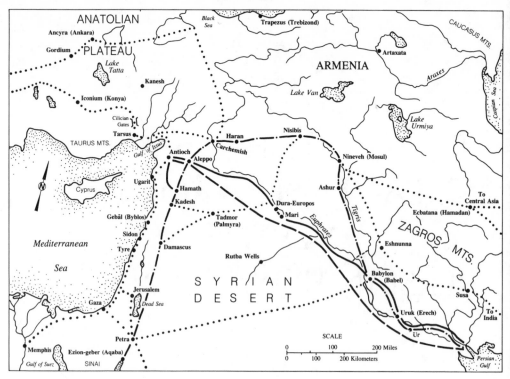

The Mesopotamian Routes in Old Testament Times

———————— Great Desert Route (Early)   · · · · · · · Main Connecting Route

— — — Great Desert Route (Medieval)   - - - - -   Median Wall

—·—·— Fertile Crescent Route

Neither snow nor rain nor heat nor gloom of night
Stays these couriers from the swift completion of their appointed
rounds.

This description was borrowed by the United States Post Office in modern times. But it was first used to describe Persian postal couriers during the fifth century B.C.! (The author was the Greek historian Herodotus.) The Persians used their Royal Road to develop the first long-distance message system. This impressive system was only the first of several networks that would bind together the countries of Western Asia and their rulers, including Greeks, Romans, Moslem Arabs, and Turks. In addition, the Persian postal system influenced the growth of the great Roman road system in the West and the Indian Grand Road in the East.

Mesopotamia: Between Two Rivers. Both the Persian Royal
Road and the Great Desert Route passed through an ancient region
called Mesopotamia. The word "Mesopotamia" means "between two
rivers." These two rivers are the Tigris and the Euphrates. This area
is located where the modern country of Iraq is today. Mesopotamia
was known as "the cradle of civilization" because scientists believe
that this is where Sumer, one of the earliest civilizations, arose.

You might think that it would be easier to travel by river than
overland in this region, especially if land routes didn't exist. But the
Tigris and Euphrates are not suitable for long-distance travel. The
Euphrates had many whirlpools, and the Tigris curls around in wide
loops. This makes it dangerous to travel downstream, and almost
impossible to travel upstream. In addition, for six months after the
winter rains, both rivers are often in flood. Floods were so frequent
that the story of a great flood, like the one in the story of Noah's
Ark, were often found in the ancient legends of this land. Noah

Tradition has it that
Noah's ark landed on
Mount Ararat, on the
Anatolian Plateau in
modern Turkey.
(Turkish Embassy Press
Department)

himself was said to have landed his ark on Mt. Ararat, which today is in the modern country of Turkey, just north of Mesopotamia.

Even during the summer months, travel downstream was slow. Early peoples sometimes sailed on inflated goatskins, which could only go as fast as the river's slow current. Such sailing was dangerous, for a goatskin could easily bump into a rock or a sandbar (a ridge of sand that had piled up underwater, out of sight, but able to scrape the bottom of a raft or boat). Travel upstream was obviously even slower.

As a result, travelers throughout history usually took the main land routes: the Great Desert Route and the Persian Royal Road.

Shifting Routes. Neither the Great Desert Route nor the Persian Royal Road followed a fixed course. These routes shifted over time. Changes in climate affected people's choice of where to go. So did changes in politics—new rulers or new uprisings that made some ways more dangerous than others.

The rivers themselves did not follow a fixed path. In the 19th century, the Tigris and the Euphrates met to form a joint mouth—the Shatt el-Arab—at the Persian Gulf. But for many centuries before that, from the time of a great flood in 629 A.D., the mouth of the Tigris lay farther to the east, while the Euphrates lay farther west. And before that, the course of the rivers is even less clear.

The Roads That Linked Western Asia. The Persian Royal Road and the Great Desert Route were both important for the role they played in tying together the region of western Asia— also known as the Middle East.

The Persian Royal Road started high up on the Anatolian plateau, in the ancient region of Anatolia. (Today, Anatolia is part of modern Turkey.) It ran between two cities that were both known for their legendary wealth. The road started in Sardis, which was once the capital of the fabulously rich King Croesus of Lydia. Croesus was a real king who ruled during the sixth century B.C. The Persian Royal Road also traveled through the city of Gordium, which was supposed to have been the home of King Midas. Midas was not a real king— only a figure in Greek mythology. He was supposed to have the power of turning everything he touched into gold.

The Persian Royal Road continued to the city of Ancyra, which has become the modern city of Ankara, capital of Turkey. Then this road cut south across the upper Euphrates and Tigris rivers, through the Persian royal capital of Susa, and on into the Persian royal summer palace at Persepolis.

The Persian Royal Road was much used throughout history. That's partly because the road ran through fertile areas that were well supplied with water. In the west, this road connected with Europe via Greece, the Danube Valley, and the Black Sea coast. In the east, it linked with an overland route to India, and with the great Silk Road that reached across Asia to China. (The Silk Road got its name from the silk merchants that traveled to and from China.)

In some periods, the Persian Royal Road was a dangerous route, however. Raiders and hill peoples often attacked travelers, especially wealthy merchants carrying rich goods. So travelers often favored a better-protected shortcut—the Great Desert Route.

The Great Desert Route ran farther west. It followed the inner curve of the so-called Fertile Crescent—the rich arc of farmland bordered by the Tigris, the Euphrates, and the Mediterranean Sea. The Great Desert Route began at the Mesopotamian ports on the Persian Gulf. From there, it ran along the edge of the Syrian Desert to the crossroads city of Aleppo, and on to the nearby Syrian ports on the Mediterranean.

The Great Desert Route and the Spice Route. Many years ago, certain goods were found only in the Far East. Many spices grew only in Indonesia, Malaysia, and the Spice Islands. Fine silks and cottons, porcelain, jewels, and certain ornaments were produced only in China and India. Trade in these Eastern goods took place along the Spice Route.

Naturally, the Europeans were eager to buy these luxury goods. But how did the goods get from the East to Europe? One major path was the Great Desert Route, which linked the Spice Route with the Mediterranean. Then Arabs in the Mediterranean would carry the goods farther west, to Europe.

Traveling in the Desert. Imagine having to cross a great desert in order to trade for precious silks, jewels, and spices. How difficult do you think such travel would be? What comes to mind when you try to picture a desert? The desert crossed by the Great Desert Route was the Syrian Desert. Many people picture this desert as a sea of sand dunes, bare and flat, except for the shifting mounds of sand blown by the wind.

In fact, this is not what the Syrian Desert looks like. The 18th-century English traveler Bartholomew Plaisted wrote: "...this desert has generally been represented as a level sandy plain; whereas in reality the greatest part is a hard sandy gravel like some of our heaths in England. In some places it is full of large loose stones, and in others full of small hills, which are more barren than the valleys or planes."

Unlike the way many people picture deserts, there was usually some water to be found in this region. But the water might not be drinkable. It was often muddy, brackish (salty), or full of algae.

Early Times

Travel and trade along the Great Desert Route and the Persian Royal Road began many thousands of years before recorded history. In those times, feet were the main means of land transportation. The only vehicles were sledges—flat boards on which goods could be piled. The sledges had to be dragged along the ground by people because the wheel had not yet been invented and no animals had yet been domesticated. Nevertheless, even in those early times, people wanted to travel and trade with each other.

Nomads. Trade along these two routes probably had its roots in the seasonal migrations of early nomads and their herds of sheep and goats. Nomads are wandering people with no permanent home. They wander with the seasons, going where there is fresh grass for their animals to eat.

As you can imagine, nomads have to travel light, for they carry with them everything they own. In early times, they would bring small, lightweight, valuable items, like gems or gold, and barter them from one region to another. To *barter* something means to make a direct trade. Since there was no system of money at this time, a nomad could not sell, say, a jewel for money. Instead, he or she would trade or *barter* it for something he or she needed, such as an animal, or a piece of woven cloth. Some nomads did carry bulkier goods. Mesopotamia was very short of materials like wood, copper, and tin. The nomads who could bring these in from other regions could receive many precious goods in return.

Increased Trade. By 3000 B.C., the wheel had been invented. This made trade and travel much easier, since goods could now be hauled rather than carried. In these very early times, the main beast of burden was the donkey. Centuries later, people learned to tame camels, which were much better suited to desert work. However, at this time, goods were usually loaded in a backpack or carried in a cart. Travelers walked beside their animals, for they had not yet learned how to ride.

Trade had advanced so far in this region that many of the earliest writings found were business records. The city of Ur, west of the Euphrates, kept records of trade in wood, copper, tin, silver, gold, and semiprecious stones like lapis lazuli and carnelian. Travel and trade in these early times was so active that many large cities had special sections where foreigners lived. There traders from other lands could live by themselves, following their own customs and speaking their own language.

Migrations. The Great Desert Route and the Persian Royal Road were also important as migration routes. From the earliest times, waves of people pushed along these natural pathways, seeking better pastures, searching for new lands to conquer, or fleeing from other races who were forcing them out from their homes.

Many different peoples lived in Mesopotamia. The Caucasians lived in the hills and plateaus around the Fertile Crescent; they originally came from the Caucasus Mountains, which today are in the Soviet Union. The Hittites came down from the steppes of Russia, sweeping through the area that today is called Turkey and pushing on into Mesopotamia. They sacked the main cities and then pulled back to northern Syria and the Armenian hills. Another

The ancient capital of the Hittites lay high on the Anatolian Plateau, among harsh, windswept hills. (From James Henry Breasted, *Ancient Times: A History of the Early World...*, 1914)

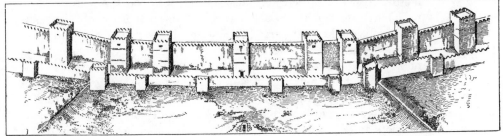

group, the Iranians, came from east of the Caspian Sea and onto the Iranian plateau. Each of these three peoples is the ancestor of a people living in the Middle East today.

CHANGING TIMES

Changing Travel: Taming the Camel. By 1300 B.C., humans began to ride animals. At first, Mesopotamian travelers rode donkeys and horses. By the 10th century B.C., they began to ride one-humped Arabian camels. These camels had been tamed by peoples on the coast of the Persian Gulf. Unlike the two-humped Bactrian camel of Central Asia, the Arabian camel was able to endure the desert. Gradually, it became the main beast of burden in Mesopotamia, especially along the Great Desert Route. Donkeys, asses, and horses were still used more often on the Persian Royal Road; that cold, rocky route was better suited to these more graceful animals who were not bothered by lower temperatures.

Camels or horses carried two types of travelers: the wealthy and powerful, who could afford these beasts, and couriers, who depended on them for their speed. Most travelers, traders, and soldiers still walked, using their animals only to carry heavy packs.

Assyrian Rule. Despite the invasions of the Iranians and the Hittites, Mesopotamia was at this time controlled by the Assyrians. The Assyrians forced the Hittites and the Iranians out of Mesopotamia, into the Anatolian mountains. To do so, they often had to create their own routes, or widen tracks that only allowed passage for one person into a road fit for an army.

That's what the Assyrian King Sargon II did in the 8th century B.C., as he pressed into the Armenian hills:

> I set out on the difficult road to Mussassir—I crossed the upper Zeb; between the high mountains, the great heights, the inaccessible mountain peaks which defy description, between them there is no path for the foot-soldiers. Mighty waterfalls rush down and the noise of their fall is like thunder....[The mountains] strike terror into those who penetrate them, where no ruler has yet set foot and whose paths no Prince who lived before me has even seen. I felled the great tree trunks and had their tall tips cut through with the bronze aces; I improved the narrow pass, through which the foot-soldiers had to force their way, and enabled the army to move on. I caused my war chariots to be hauled up with ropes and I took up my position on

horseback at the head of my army, and my warriors moved forward
slowly and in single file with their horses....

To us, the Armenian highlands might not look very high, for they
were only 5,000-6,000 feet high. But the Assyrians lived near sea
level. Even though Sargon may have been exaggerating, he and his
men must have been impressed by the rocky heights.

The Medes and the Persians.   Around the seventh century B.C.,
the balance of power in the region began to change. The Iranians
comprised two main groups, the Medes and the Persians. The Medes
started out as the stronger of the two, and they began to press
westward. The Assyrians even built a wall between the Euphrates
and the Tigris to keep them out.

But the Medes made one fatal mistake: they overestimated their
own strength. They over-stretched themselves in going too far west
and could not control other invading peoples coming across the
Caucasus.

As a result, the Persians gained the upper hand. They set up a
stronghold along the Persian Gulf. Then they gradually took over
the lands that the Medes held. Under Cyrus the Great in the mid-
sixth century B.C., the Persians controlled the largest empire the

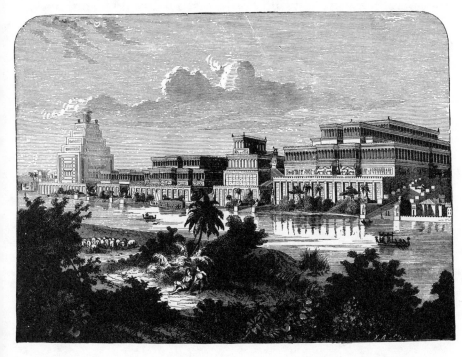

At the height of their
power, the Assyrians
built great palaces, like
this one—an artist's
reconstruction—for
their king, Sennacherib.
(From L. W. Yaggy and
T. L. Haines, *Museum
of Antiquity,* 1882)

world had yet known: from Central Asia through Mesopotamia, Egypt, and Anatolia (Turkey), and on into Greece. The next Persian king, Darius, ruled this gigantic empire. And he became famous in his own right as the creator of the Persian Royal Road.

THE ROYAL ROAD AND THE PERSIAN EMPIRE

Darius saw clearly that his vast empire needed good communications to survive. He had to be able to communicate with all the governors and military leaders in all his lands in order to maintain tight control of all his territories. But in those days, communication depended entirely on messengers carrying messages from one place to another.

Swift travel requires good roads, which are well marked and well protected from robbers and raiders. The Persian Royal Road was such a road—and it did make travel faster. Darius's road enabled him to send messages from the Persian capital of Susa to the Anatolian city of Sardis in nine days. A message from Susa to the Mediterranean seaports of Smyrna or Ephesus (both in modern-day Turkey) took only 10 days. Even Darius's Greek enemies admired his Royal Road.

Darius had a clever way of sending messages along this road. One courier, or messenger, would ride as fast as he could for one day. At

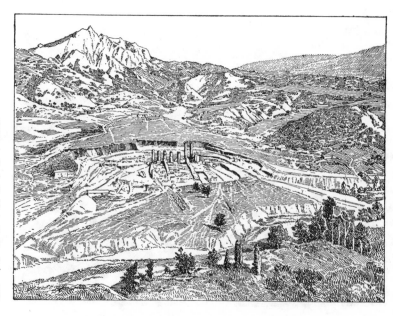

Modern archaeologists have discovered through their excavations many of the secrets of the city of Sardis, once capital of the immensely rich King Croesus and the endpoint of the Persian Royal Road. (From James Henry Breasted, *Ancient Times: A History of the Early World,* 1914)

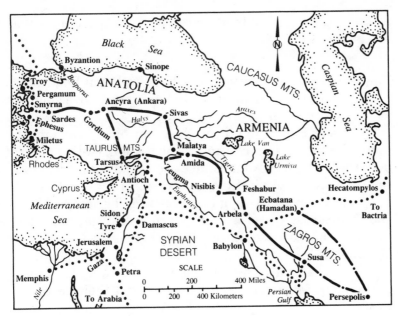

The Persian Royal Road

———————— Persian Royal Road

—— · —— · —— Other Main Persian Routes

· · · · · · · · · · Main Connecting Land Routes

the end of the day's travel, he would have reached a second courier, who would be well rested and have a fresh, well rested horse; this second courier would continue on with the message. The second courier would pass on the message to a third, and so on until the message reached its destination.

The Persian Royal Road comprised some sections of earlier roads, yet it was unique in being a road built for long-distance purposes. Like modern freeways, Darius's road often bypassed major cities, to avoid the hustle and bustle of city life.

The actual path taken by the Persian Royal road changed over time. However, it continued to be a fast road, which could be covered in nine or ten days for a swift courier and perhaps three months for a traveler on foot or as part of a caravan. A caravan is a group of travelers traveling with pack animals and carrying goods for trade. A caravan must carry enough supplies to be able to sustain all the people and animals for their long journeys across the desert.

Many people did use the Royal Road at this slower pace. Eventually, way stations were established along the road, which were places which supplied fresh water, food, and perhaps a place to stay for the night.

The Great Desert Route. The Persian Royal Road was first and foremost a government road. Soldiers and government workers made up the larger part of its traffic.

The Great Desert Route, on the other hand, was more of a trade route. When Persians controlled the Persian Gulf, more trade came from the east, both by land and by sea. And these traders then used camel caravans to continue westward. This period saw the rise of the great caravan cities of Syria, especially Aleppo, Hama, Homs, and Damascus. These cities received goods that had been brought in from the Incense Road of Arabia, as well as the routes of Mesopotamia. Canaanites—also known as Phoenicians—and Greeks also appeared in the region, for they were building up a busy trade in the Mediterranean. They brought their goods in from the west.

ALEXANDER THE GREAT AND THE GREEK EMPIRE

In the spring of 334 B.C., a 22-year-old prince from Macedon (today part of Greece, Yugoslavia and Bulgaria) left his home, leading a Macedonian and Greek army. The prince, whose name was Alexander, was seeking to conquer lands in the East. He won his first battle against the Persians and gained control of several Greek cities from them along the west coast of Anatolia (Turkey).

Alexander's Empire Grows. Alexander went on to conquer the Persians in a long series of battles. In 332 he founded Alexandria in Egypt, the most famous of the many cities that were named after him. Then he turned his attention once more toward western Asia, where he again fought the Persians.

In the spring of 331 B.C., Alexander marched north from Damascus, then east. He crossed the wide upper Euphrates on a specially built pontoon bridge—that is, a bridge that rests on barrels floating in the water.

When Alexander came to the upper Tigris, he again faced the difficult problem of how to get his army across. The upper Tigris was a fast-moving river, and Alexander was afraid that the swift current might knock his men over and sweep them away.

He solved the problem in an ingenious way. He had rows of cavalry—soldiers on horses—stand right in the river. This made the swift current flow more slowly and gently, as it swirled around the horses' legs. That way, the infantry soldiers—or foot soldiers—could cross the river more easily, wading between the horses.

Once again, Greeks and Persians fought. And once again, even though the Persian king Darius had the larger army, he lost to Alexander and his army. Darius fled for his life, this time into the Iranian hills. With the Persian army broken, Alexander continued his conquests. He moved through the fertile plains and rich cities of Mesopotamia, including Babylon and Susa, removing Persian lords and putting his own men in their place.

During this campaign, the Greeks were often stunned by Persian wealth and culture. They were never more stunned than at Persepolis, which drew on the best of the Mesopotamian, Indian, and Greek cultures. Even though Alexander admired Persian culture, he decided to burn the great palace, destroying it forever.

From Persepolis, Alexander launched his Asiatic campaign, enlarging his empire to include the region known today as Afghanistan, and invading India. Finally, 11,000 miles from their home, Alexander's soldiers would not go on and he returned to Persia with them, dying two years later.

This partial reconstruction of an ancient mural shows Alexander (left) and Darius (right of center, in the chariot) at the Battle of Issus. (From James Henry Breasted, *Ancient Times: A History of the Early World...*, 1914)

By accident or design, Alexander the Great's army destroyed the great Persian summer palace at Persepolis, leaving only these ruins. (From James Henry Breasted, *Ancient Times: A History of the Early World...*, 1914)

After Alexander. Even after Alexander's death, Greeks remained in Mesopotamia. Trade and travel grew even more than before. Goods from Syria passed along the Mesopotamian routes and beyond, even into India and Central Asia, possibly as far as China.

With Alexander, travel on the Persian Royal Road had decreased. Instead, the Great Desert Route—the shortcut between the Persian Gulf and the Mediterranean—had become Mesopotamia's main road. After Alexander, however, the Desert Route became unsafe in places. As a result, many travelers reverted to the Persian Royal Road, even though it was somewhat less convenient than the desert shortcut.

THE ROMAN EMPIRE

Just as the Greek empire under Alexander had been larger than the Persian Empire, so the Roman Empire was destined to grow larger than that of Alexander. Part of Roman expansion was into Asia. The Romans took control of most of Asia Minor, upper Mesopotamia, and a wide stretch from northern Syria down to Arabia and Egypt.

The Romans and others fought a series of border wars during this expansion period, and so the Great Desert Route and the Persian Royal Road became unsafe and were therefore used less often. When peace was finally established, just before the first century A.D., both routes were bypassed. The Romans chose to move traffic straight across the Syrian Desert, so that they could pass through the oasis of Palmyra.

The Romans are famous for their excellent road-building skills, and they made this new desert route usable for people on very long journeys. They sank wells, so that water would be available along the way. They built forts, to help protect merchants against robbers and raiders. As a result, caravan travel increased and the city of Palmyra flourished.

CARAVAN DAYS: CONNECTIONS WITH CHINA AND INDIA

These were the great early days of the Silk Road, the road along which merchants traded for China's famous silks. Rome and China traded with each other across the continent of Asia, and both traded with India as well.

Palmyra: The Crossroads City. Palmyra was the crossroads of this three-way trade. Hundreds of stone columns lined the road that led into the great city. Many of these columns are still standing today. In the center of the city were the caravanserais, the all-pur-

Ruined columns open to the sky are all that remain of Palmyra, once the crossroads of the Syrian Desert. (Iraq Petroleum Company)

pose quarters where travelers could rest and store their goods. There was also a temple, which was probably already old by Roman times. The temple was dedicated to Arsu and Azizu, the gods of the caravaners.

The caravan trade made the people of Palmyra wealthy and powerful. Many became respected Roman citizens. Palmyrene traders spread as far as Egypt, the Danube, and Rome, where they had a temple dedicated to their own special gods.

Palmyra's heyday lasted into the third century A.D. Then its queen, Zenobia, tried to break completely free of the Roman Empire. Rome was vengeful. The empire not only defeated Zenobia, but it also destroyed her city.

Although during this period, the main trade route crossed through Palmyra, other routes in western Anatolia (Turkey) also flourished under the Romans. They saw a stream of traders and soldiers, whose travels linked together the different parts of the Roman Empire.

The Spread of Christianity. The Anatolian routes carried some of the earliest and most important Christian missionaries. One of the most important of these early missionaries was St. Paul, who was born in Tarsus, in Asia Minor. Early on in his life, Paul, known then as Saul, had been a Roman official. He was on his way to Damascus, in Syria, to arrest some Christians, when he had a vision that caused him to take a new religion—Christianity—and a new name—Paul. Paul then traveled throughout the region: to Antioch, Damascus, Jerusalem, Ephesus (in Greece), and Troas (the Turkish region around the once-great city of Troy). Paul preached his religion wherever he went.

Eventually, some centuries later, the Romans adopted Christianity as their official religion. This happened under the Emperor Constantine, in the fourth century A.D. Constantine also shifted the center of the Roman Empire from Rome to the Eastern city of Byzantium, which he renamed Constantinople. (Today the city is named Istanbul, and is located in the modern country of Turkey.)

After this shift, the Western Roman Empire—the lands that were west of Constantinople—began to decline. The old main roads leading west to Greece out of Asia were much less used. Never again would they be as important as they were in Roman times. Instead, the main road went north from Tarsus through Iconium (the modern city of Konya) to Constantinople. The Eastern Roman Empire, also known as the Byzantine Empire, thrived and continued to trade vigorously with other lands.

MOSLEM TIMES: THE ARABS' EMPIRE

Islam: A New World Religion. In the seventh century A.D., a new religion known as Islam, was founded. The followers of Islam are known as Moslems. This new religion spread quickly from Mecca, in Saudi Arabia, where it was founded, throughout the Middle East. By the late eighth century, the Moslems had founded their own capital, Baghdad, at the ancient "waist" of Mesopotamia, where the Tigris and Euphrates draw near each other. Today Baghdad is the capital of Iraq.

The Moslems Expand. In the ninth century, the Moslems spread north to Tarsus and on to the foothills of the Taurus Mountains, the Armenian highlands, and the Caucasus Mountains. With all of Syria and Mesopotamia under their control, the Moslems built a strong trading empire.

The Europeans relied upon the Moslems to bring goods from China, India, and the Far East. The Moslems traded with the East for spices, silks, cottons, porcelain, and other goods that could not be found in Europe. Then they brought those goods west to the Mediterranean, from where they reached the countries of France,

Approaching Antioch from Aleppo, the Great Desert Route passed through protective coastal mountains. (From Douglas Carruthers, *The Desert Route to India*)

Italy, and Spain. In Europe, the Moslems came to be known as "Saracens."

Moslem Caravans. Between the eighth and the 11th centuries, Moslem caravans on the Mesopotamian routes began to take the form they still have in modern times. Merchants and other travelers would join together in caravans under an elected leader called a *bashi*. The bashi was almost always an Arab sheik, or leader.

The bashi would oversee the two to three months of preparation needed for a large caravan—choosing the camels, buying and packing the food and water, and doing all the other things necessary to help several people travel through the desert. The bashi also had to pay tribute to the peoples the caravan encountered along the route, to ensure a safe journey. The bashi had to find out how much to pay, and to whom, although all the members of the caravan shared in the final expense.

A bashi also hired a special guide, called a *daleel*, as well as couriers, who were called *basheers* if they brought good news and *nadeers* if they brought bad news. The couriers could move more quickly than the rest of the caravan, so they could bring back news about where it was safe to travel. Caravans also included a religious leader, called a *muezzin*, and a *kahweji*, who made and distributed coffee on the trip. There was also the *bayrakdar*, who carried the caravan's flag at the head of the line.

Few Christians found their way onto the Mesopotamian routes in these early Moslem times. But Jewish traders—some from distant parts of Europe—would often join Moslem caravans. They would often bribe the caravan leader to set up camp on the Jewish Sabbath, since Orthodox Jews are not allowed to ride animals on this day. Or, if the caravan leader would not stop the whole group, the Jewish merchants might have to hire a special escort to help protect them, so that they could ride ahead of the others, in order to reach their destination before the Sabbath; or so that they could catch up with the caravan after the day of rest was over. This meant that Jewish merchants usually took the Persian Royal Road, even though it was longer, so that they would not have to travel alone in the dangerous desert.

For other travelers, the Great Desert Route was the more convenient, and so it became the main route. It was a great highway between the Mediterranean Sea and the Persian Gulf, especially as Moslem power grew in both regions.

The Caravans Choose a Path. The general course followed by any caravan was determined by the oases along the route. Caravans depended on these protected places, where they could rest in the shade of palm trees, find fresh water, and perhaps buy food or other supplies from those who lived there.

The Pigeon Post. The Moslems also maintained the postal system set up by the Persians and carried on by the Greeks, the Romans, and the Byzantines. In the eighth century, the Moslems set up their postal system along the Persian Royal Road route from Baghdad, going toward Aleppo. By the ninth century, the system had linked up with a similar system based in Damascus. This system worked very well through the 11th century. The *Sahib el-Beric*, chief of the postal system, also became unofficial chief of all Moslem provincial (or regional) officials.

But the regular postal system was not enough. Communications along the Great Desert Route were so important that the Moslems set up a pigeon post between the two ends of the route.

Pigeon towers were placed every 50 miles or so along the way. A pigeon wearing a message tied to its leg would fly from one tower to the next, where someone would remove the message and tie it onto a new pigeon. With pigeon relays, a message might reach from one end of the route to the other in a few days, rather than in the weeks or months that a caravan would take.

This pigeon post worked for over a thousand years. Finally, in the mid-18th century, it was closed down for unknown reasons. Rumor had it that a pigeon died or was killed, and a message fell into the wrong hands, but nobody really knows for sure.

Until that time, however, Basra and Iskanderun carrier pigeons were famous throughout the Western world. Merchant caravans on the Great Desert Route often carried homing pigeons with them. Homing pigeons are birds that are able to find their way back to a particular place. Caravans could release a homing pigeon from Aleppo or Basra in order to let people in that city know their location, and to warn others of any trouble on the road.

The Seljuk Turks. In the early 11th century, travel in the region was upset. A new group, the Seljuk Turks, was pressing into Iran from Mesopotamia. The Seljuk Turks were newly converted Moslems, and they were out to convert everyone else to their religion.

The Byzantine army, protecting their Eastern Orthodox Christian empire, just barely managed to hold back the Seljuk Turks at the Taurus Mountains. Many Armenians fled from these Turks, but later found themselves surrounded. The Seljuk Turks swept through all of Anatolia except for the coastal strip across from Constantinople.

At this time the Byzantine Empire was very weak. Thus, the Seljuk Turks were able to take control of the city of Jerusalem. This city was considered holy by the Christians, and until the Seljuk Turks came into the region, Christians had been free to make religious journeys, or pilgrimages, to Jerusalem. But the Seljuk Turks decided not to allow Christians through their territory.

The Byzantines called on the Europeans for help, appealing to the Catholic Church as well as to European governments. This marked the beginning of the period of the Crusades, or religious wars, in which Europeans tried to conquer the Seljuk Turks and remove them from their lands in the Middle East.

In earlier centuries, the Byzantine Empire had kept the roads in Anatolia in a good state of repair for their own postal system and trading caravans. But 20 years of battle with the Seljuk Turks had left their highways in very poor shape. Steven Runciman describes what the Crusaders found as they crossed from Constantinople toward Antioch:

> It was now early October, and the autumn rains had begun. The road over the Anti-Taurus was in appalling disrepair; and for miles there was only a muddy path leading up steep inclines and skirting precipices. Horse after horse slipped and fell over the edge; whole lines of baggage animals, roped together, dragged each other down into the abyss. No one dared to ride. The knights, struggling on foot under their heavy accoutrements [gear], eagerly tried to sell their arms to more lightly equipped men, or threw them away in disrepair. The mountains were accursed...

The Crusaders and the Byzantine army took back control of parts of Anatolia and set up several Christian states along the Mediterranean. Jewish merchants were soon acting as middlemen along the Great Desert Route. To the Christians, they supplied the goods that the Moslems had brought from China, India, and the Far East. The most eager customers for these goods were the Italians, especially those from the cities of Venice, Genoa, and Pisa. These cities were handling more and more trade on the Mediterranean (see Chapter 3).

The sack of Baghdad by the Mongols in 1258 was as shocking to the Islamic world as the sack of Rome was to Europe. (From Rashid ad-Din, *University History*, late 14th century, MS. suppl. pers. 1113f. 180v-181r, Bibliothèque Nationale, Paris)

THE MONGOLS AND THEIR EMPIRE

The Near East then faced a new powerful force from the outside: the Mongols. This people came from the Asian region that we now know as Mongolia. They shocked the Moslem world by sacking—or robbing—the great city of Baghdad in 1258.

The Mongol invasion changed the shape of the Moslem world. The center of Moslem power shifted to Cairo, the capital of today's Egypt. Meanwhile, the Mongols took much of the land around the Great Desert Route and the Persian Royal Road. They conquered territories from Mesopotamia all the way east to the China Sea. The centuries of war on the great trade routes led trade and travel to drop to its lowest point ever.

A New Time of Trade. But once the Mongols were firmly in power, the situation changed. They then brought peace and free trade to their new empire. Moslem traders once again traveled the Mesopotamian routes to Basra, the Persian Gulf port, and the Spice Route to the East. Others went overland to China. This was a unique time in human history. Only under the Mongols— from the mid-13th to the mid-14th centuries—were people able to travel all across Asia on the Great Silk Road. In this period, the Great Desert Route

During the Mongol period, traders from Central Asia would often pick up the route of the old Persian Royal Road, passing through Armenian towns like this one to the Black Sea. (From *Livre des Merveilles,* 1375, MS. Fr. 2810, f. 7, Bibliothèque Nationale)

and the Persian Royal Road became in effect extensions of the Silk Road.

Decline of the Mongols. Then, in the late 14th century, the Mongols lost control of Asia. The Great Desert Route became the preferred highway, for it was best protected from the warring powers in the East. During this period, many Europeans moved into the Middle Eastern trade. Italians from the cities of Venice, Pisa, and Genoa, as well as Catalans from the Spanish city of Barcelona, set up warehouses in the main Syrian cities, as well as in the seaports of Beirut (in today's Lebanon) and Tripoli (in today's Libya).

THE OTTOMAN TURKS AND THE OTTOMAN EMPIRE

The Fall of the Byzantine Empire. By the end of the 15th century, the Christian Byzantine Empire was extremely weak. It was no match for the last great wave of Central Asian invaders: the Ottoman Turks. This new people moved swiftly across Anatolia and took the capital city of Constantinople in 1453. This effectively meant the end of the Byzantine Empire and the beginning of a new powerful empire—the Ottoman Empire.

This empire was extended as the Ottoman Turks reached south toward the Mediterranean Sea. By 1600, their lands reached to

Belgrade (in modern Yugoslavia) and Odessa (in the modern Ukraine, of the Soviet Union) in Europe; Basra in Mesopotamia; Mecca in Arabia (in today's Saudi Arabia); and Cairo (in Egypt) and Algiers (in today's Algeria) in northern Africa.

European Response. While the Ottomans were building their empire, they almost put a stop to Eastern trade with Europe. The effect was earth-shaking. As we have seen, Europeans depended on the Moslems of the Middle East to bring them goods from the Far East that they could not grow or make themselves. They did not want to be cut off from these goods—so they decided to explore new routes to the East themselves.

The Portuguese slowly made their way around the continent of Africa, learning its shape and finding the Cape of Good Hope Route to India and China. The Spanish sent Italian sailor Christopher Columbus west, hoping that sooner or later, he would sail round the world to reach the East. Instead, Columbus discovered the continents of North and South America, which opened up new sources of wealth for the Europeans.

As a result of new European exploration efforts, the Great Desert Route, which had been used to bring goods from the East, was barely used during a large part of the 16th century. However, tiny Portugal (the main trading nation) could not handle all of the Eastern trade by itself, and Moslems were soon trading again at Basra.

Courier Services by Christians and Moslems. As trade revived, European Christians began to join Moslems and Jews on the Great Desert Route. At first they were not traders, but couriers. The Portuguese began this dangerous overland courier service for important messages to and from businesspeople in the East. They realized that the sea route—by way of Africa's Cape of Good Hope—could take as long as 24 months for sending a message and receiving a reply.

The Ottoman Turks built their own courier service to replace the older Moslem postal system. These couriers were given strict deadlines. They were expected to push on quickly, picking up fresh horses at relay stations. European observers reported that the highest-level couriers, those who traveled on the most important government business, could cover the 1,400-1,500 mile distance between Baghdad and Constantinople in just 12 or 13 days.

The British and Their Companies. In the early 1600s, other Europeans began to build new empires in the East. Most used the Cape of Good Hope Route around Africa, and many European colonies were founded on the coast along the route. But other European powers settled on the Mediterranean coast and set up companies in this area—at the ends of the overland routes from the East. The British, for example, set up the Levant Company in 1605. They sent representatives to protect the interests of British merchants in many Near Eastern cities, including Aleppo, Tripoli, Smyrna, and Constantinople.

British power in India was also increasing. The British therefore needed their own overland courier system, to allow business and government communication between these Eastern lands. They made good use of the Great Desert Route between Basra and Aleppo.

The Dangers of the Overland Routes. European traders and travelers in this period also began crossing Asia on the Great Desert Route from Aleppo to Basra. They made these crossings with the large merchant *kafilas*, an Arabic word for "companies of people and camels." But the Ottoman Turks took so much in taxes that the European merchants found overland trade unprofitable. Even the long and expensive sea voyage to the East was less costly.

Worse than that, the overland routes were unsafe. Desert Arabs fighting Turkish rule often attacked travelers. The Turks were also troubled by rebellions in major cities, such as Aleppo, Baghdad, and Basra. The overland routes became so dangerous that for almost a century—between 1663 and 1745—no Europeans are known to have used them.

The Return of the Europeans. By the 1740s, the region was more peaceful. Europeans once again used the Great Desert Route as a shortcut to the East. The most frequent users were British and French travelers. Both Britain and France had expanded their colonies in Asia and Africa, so many businesspeople and government officials had business in these areas. Couriers, merchants, and plain adventurers could all be found along the Great Desert Route.

This route was still the safest of the overland routes in the region. However, it still was not totally secure. Caravans had to pay tolls to the various sheiks, or leaders, along the way. Even so, they often met with wild bands of raiders who had not been paid off. They had to hire extra guards for protection. The caravan leader himself might also demand extra money from strangers once the caravan had left and the stranger was stuck in the desert.

CARAVAN LIFE

The caravans themselves were often very large. Sometimes they had as many as 2,000 camels. Such massive journeys required a substantial amount of preparation from travelers. They had to rent camels and perhaps also litters—covered couches carried by camels or people, in which a traveler could ride.

Travelers also hired servants to care for their camels and prepare their food. The camels had to be supplied with skins full of water, and with adequate food—usually rice, bread, coffee, and ghee (boiled butter). The camels and other animals traveling with the caravan also had to be fed. Usually, however, they would find their own food along the route. The people would also hunt fresh game, such as gazelles, hares, and birds to supplement their supplies. They might even also eat caravan animals that weakened and died, including camels and donkeys. In addition, people in the caravan had to keep a lookout for dangerous animals along the way, including wolves, foxes, tigers, and lions.

Travelers carried tents for themselves and their servants. Europeans also often carried cots. According to the 18th-century English traveler William Beawes, they made the cots "stand a more than ordinary distance from the ground, as a security from the snakes and scorpions that are common it seems in the desert." The tents, wrote Beawes, were best pitched "somewhat apart from and to windward of the rest of the caravans, as else at the time of cooking you are molested with smoke and also with dust from the camels continually rambling about you."

Dust on the road was also a problem. Here's a description by another European traveler, Bartholomew Plaisted, writing in 1750:

> ...the north-west wind...blows directly in your face, and is as violent as if it came from a glass furnace, and penetrates into your very lungs...The Arabs turn a part of their turbant [turban] before their mouth and nostrils, by which they find a small alleviation. It likewise greatly affects the eyes; which perhaps might be remedied by green glass, worn like spectacles, and tied behind the head to keep them fast....

Many travelers on the Great Desert Route stopped at Meshed Ali, or Najaf, tomb of the founder of the Moslem Shi'a sect. (From Douglas Carruthers, *The Desert Route to India*)

The pattern of the day varied with the size of the caravan and the decisions of the all-powerful leader. For Beawes's caravan, the day shaped up like this:

> The order for diet in the caravan is coffee in the morning before mounting; then when they stop about noon for an hour coffee again and what else any has ready drest; in the evening it is pleasant for anyone to observe soon after encamping there appears almost as many fires as men and all hands set to preparing…what…their stores may afford.…

The traveling day would often last for 12 or 13 hours, starting around dawn. It might go even longer than expected, if the oasis where the caravan had planned to stop turned out not to have enough water for the thousands of people and animals.

The caravan leader made all the major decisions about the caravan, according to the *rafeek* system. The caravan leader paid the ruling local sheik, who then sent along a member of his nation, called a *rafeek*. He rode at the front of the caravan and carried his sheik's flag. He was like a signal to all that the caravan should not be interfered with by any who respected the sheik.

The Arabian people had a long, strong set of alliances among themselves. So this system worked rather well in settled times, and it reduced the need for hundreds of expensive armed guards to protect the caravans from desert people. In troubled times, however, the system broke down, for then the different desert peoples were warring among themselves. Then the caravan needed armed guards to guarantee its safety. Sometimes these guards would be hired in the territories it was passing through.

Melons, dates, and fresh meats were sometimes bought from villages along the route. Travelers might spend the night in rest houses provided by charities, but perhaps they were more comfortable out in the desert! Beawes found the heat of the day very tiring—but at night, camping under the stars, it was "so cool that quilt double was scarce sufficient to keep me warm."

The last part of the trip was usually considered the worst part of the journey. From the town of Meshed Ali to Basra, Beawes found that "...the country [was] exceedingly bare and sandy; the weather hotter and the water tho' frequent [was] very brackish [half fresh and half salt], and foul in most places, which often disorder[ed] our bowels and occasion[ed] severe sickness of the stomach."

For large merchant caravans, the whole trip between Aleppo and Basra—750 to 800 miles—took anywhere from 30 to 70 days, depending on road conditions and the route taken. Then, what travelers found in Basra depended largely on the time of the year. The city came fully alive only in those months when Spice Route ships had sailed up the Persian Gulf. These ships could only come

The city of Aleppo was built on eight small hills, with a castle on the highest of them. (From Douglas Carruthers, *The Desert Route to India*)

during certain months of the year, which depended on the season. They had to time their voyages so that they would be in port during the storms. Therefore, the large merchant caravans also tried to time themselves to meet these ships. However, such timing could not always be controlled.

Sometimes travelers tried to cross the desert by themselves—but they had good reason to avoid doing so whenever possible. More than one traveler had arrived in a Mesopotamian city wearing only newspaper. Everything else—including the shirt off his back—had been stolen along the way!

Suez and Afterward

During the 18th and 19th centuries, the British continued to expand their power in India and in the Middle East. They were particularly strong in Egypt. As their power grew, the short overland route at Suez came to be used more than the Great Desert Route.

The Suez Canal. Suez, an important port since the 18th century, became even more important after the opening of the Suez Canal in 1869. This canal connects the Red Sea with the Mediterranean. It made East-West trade faster and easier, changing travel patterns in the region forever.

The Suez Canal is located in Egypt, and was originally built by a private company in which European countries held the major shares. Eventually, it came to be controlled by Great Britain. Because of this, British power in Egypt grew even more in the years after the canal was opened.

Modern Times

One major change that has occurred in modes of travel in modern times has been the invention of the automobile. Motor vehicles suddenly made desert travel far faster and, therefore, safer. British and later U.S. experts used cars and trucks to search for oil in Middle Eastern deserts. Much later, cars took second place to airplanes, which could cross the desert even more easily. Even if the desert were now controlled by several different countries, an airplane could fly over their boundaries to reach its far-off destination.

Many merchants waited for word of their Mediterranean ships in the mountain retreat of Antioch, Syria, shown here just before World War I. (From James Henry Breasted, *Ancient Times: A History of the Early World...*, 1914)

In our own time, the great road system of the past has fallen apart. It is still used for local purposes by old vehicles and by the still-present camels in the desert, and by donkeys in the mountains. But to follow Abraham's or Alexander's path today would be quite difficult. To cross the borders of Iran, Iraq, Syria, and Turkey would require many visas and much negotiation with the officials of these rival countries.

Even apart from the political problems, travel in this region is still not easy. Evelyn Lyle describes a bus trip in the mid-1960s on what had been the old main route heading south, down from the 5,000-foot high Anatolian plateau:

> The road worsened as we climbed into valleys filled with giant boulders often higher than the bus itself. Once or twice the bus squeezed through between rocks towering above it, with merely a fraction of an inch to spare; it was easy to believe that this was the original caravan road of the past few thousand years.

Most of Anatolia and Mesopotamia is no longer set up for long-distance travelers. The traveler may find little food and water beyond that provided by tent restaurants set up along the way, and generally he or she has to sleep in or near the bus or truck. Unlike centuries past, there are no welcoming villages to await the modern traveler at the end of each day's journey.

Carruthers, Douglas, ed. *The Desert Route to India: Being the Journals of Four Travellers by the Great Desert Caravan Between Aleppo and Basra, 1745-1751* (London: Hakluyt Society, 1929). Series II, Vol. LXIII.

Grant, Christina Phelps. *The Syrian Desert: Caravans, Travel and Exploration* (New York: Macmillan, 1938).

Hitti, Philip K. *The Near East in History: A 5000 Year Story* (Princeton, New Jersey: D. Van Nostrand, 1961).

Hoskins, Halford Lancaster. *British Routes to India* (New York: Octagon Books, 1966), reprint of 1928 edition.

Lyle, Evelyn. *The Search for the Royal Road* (London: Vision, 1966).

Rostovtzeff, M. *Caravan Cities* (Oxford: Clarendon, 1932).

Stark, Freya. *Alexander's Path: From Caria to Cilicia* (New York: Harcourt, Brace, 1958).

5

THE
INDIAN GRAND ROAD

THE ROAD THAT LEADS TO THE RICHES OF INDIA

When spring-time flushes the desert grass,
Our kafilas [caravans] wind through the Khyber Pass.
Lean are the camels but fat the frails [baskets],
Light are the purses but heavy the bales,
As the snowbound trade of the North comes down
To the market-square of Peshawur town.

In a turquoise twilight, crisp and chill,
A kafila camped at the foot of the hill.
Then blue smoke-haze of the cooking rose,
And tent-peg answered to hammer-noise;
And the picketed ponies, shag and wild,
Strained at their ropes as the feed was piled,
And the bubbling camels beside the load
Sprawled for a furlong adown the road;
And the Persian pussy-cats, brought for sale,
Spat at the dogs from the camel-bale;
And the tribesmen bellowed to hasten the food;
And the camp-fires twinkled by Fort Jumrood;
And there fled on the wings of the gathering dusk
A savour of camels and carpets of musk,
A murmur of voices, a reek of smoke,
To tell us the trade of the Khyber woke.

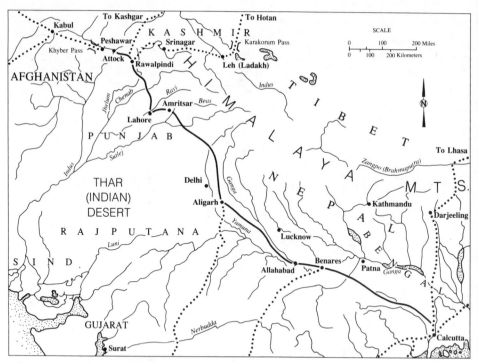

The Grand Trunk Road in 19th-Century India

———— Grand Trunk Road   · · · · · · Other Main Connecting Routes

That was the way Rudyard Kipling saw the trade of northwestern India in his poem "The Ballad of the King's Jest," which he wrote in 1890. And that was the way it had been for thousands of years.

To the unknowing traveler, the mountain passes guarding India might seem very hard to cross—cold and bare in winter, parched in autumn. Yet they have always come alive in the spring, when the melting snow and rains bring food for pack animals and water for all. These passes did not bar the way to India. They were, in fact, part of one of the world's major routes: the Indian Grand Road. This road saw many traders—and also many pilgrims, wandering theater companies, students, horse traders, tourists, and, always, invaders.

These people had many reasons for coming to India. The legendary riches of this great country have always inspired dreams of great wealth. As the medieval Arab trader Hazrat Oman put it: "The Indian rivers are pearls, the mountains rubies, and trees perfumes."

Religion also brought outsiders to India. The Buddhist religion was founded here, and India's Buddhist shrines drew devout pilgrims, or religious travelers, for thousands of years. Also founded in India were the Hindu and the Jain religions, and pilgrims came to visit their shrines as well.

Some outsiders came to India with dreams of conquest. If invaders were able to cross India's mountain passes, they might find a rich and beautiful land. Over the centuries, India was invaded by Aryans, Persians, Greeks under Alexander the Great, Huns, Islamic Turks, and Mongols. All traveled the Indian Grand Road, from the country's northwest frontier across its dusty plains all the way to the sacred Ganges River, which Indians called the Ganga.

The story of the Indian Grand Road is the story of India itself, its growth from a collection of scattered villages into a powerful nation ruled by powerful dynasties, sometimes from India itself, sometimes from foreign nations. For many years, India was ruled by the British, as one of the colonies of the British Empire. Throughout India's history, through the independent India of today, the Indian Grand Road has played a vital part in linking together the many regions of India.

NORTHERN INDIA

The Indian Grand Road runs through north India. North India is a great single plain, bounded on the north and west by an arc of mountains. Directly north, the great mountain range of the Himalayas blocks entrance into India. The world's highest mountains, Mount Everest and K2, are part of this range. Behind the Himalayas is the high Tibetan plateau. To the east, India is protected by dense, matted jungle. This jungle prevented the creation of a major land route between India and its neighbors, Burma and China.

To the south of India, of course, is the Indian Ocean. Thus there is only one way to approach India by land—from the northwest. This road leads from inner Asia to India—but even this road is very mountainous. The ranges northwest of India were not easy to cross. It was necessary to find a series of passes. These mountains are not the huge, snow-covered mountains travelers write about—and which modern mountain climbers still love and fear. Instead, these northwest mountains are considered by many the ugliest in the world. The Indian historian Moti Chandra said, "It lacks any trace of vegetation and the accumulation of ice does not enhance beauty, because there is scanty snowfall."

Below these ugly mountains, however, are India's beautiful plains. These are traversed by two great river systems. One is the Indus, or "Lion" River, which cuts down from the Himalayas. The other is the Ganges, or "Peacock" River, which drains the southern flank of the Himalayas. These rivers snake through the plains as they run to the sea on the west and the east. Between these rivers the land varied, but was often desert.

THE GEOGRAPHY OF THE ROUTE

Early travelers to India came from Mesopotamia—the area that is now part of Iraq—and Persia—the area that is now part of Iran. Travelers from China and Central Asia also came to India, but they had to circle around the high Himalayas. All these travelers had to find the mountain passes in the northwest. These passes include

From the Bamyan Valley northwest of the Indian Grand Road, Afghan nomads file toward Kabul as of old. (Delia and Ferdinand Kuhn)

the Kohat Pass, at the southern end of the range; the Malakand, at the northern end; and the famous Khyber Pass, at the western end. These routes all feed into the Kabul River Valley, where India's Grand Road began.

The Grand Road followed the Kabul River to the Indus River, and then on to the market town of Taxila. There it was joined by routes from the high passes—some as high as 19,000 feet—from Kashmir and the Karakorum (Black Gravel) Mountains to the north. Then the road crossed the rivers of the Punjab—the north Indian region whose name means "five rivers." Beyond that, the road finally reached the Ganges River and followed it east to the Bay of Bengal. There it connected with two routes to China.

This route was not one fixed path. There were shifts in some parts of it from time to time, as different cities gained power and thus diverted the route through themselves. But the Indian Grand Road has followed this basic line throughout its history.

EARLY TIMES

Around the Indus River. The earliest Indian cultures that reached a high level of development seem to have grown up along the lower Indus River, especially in the cities of Mohenjodara and Harappa. Almost 5,000 years ago, Indian peoples were trading with Mesopotamia, by land and also by sea, along the Persian Gulf that ran between them.

For reasons that we do not know, this culture reached a great height and then faded. Some time after 2000 B.C., Aryan peoples invaded it from the northwest. The Aryans were a warlike people that originally lived in southern Russia and Turkestan.

Two Groups of Aryans. There were two groups of Aryan invaders. One stayed in the Iranian plateau, to found the Persian culture and become the ancestors of the modern-day Iranians. The other group moved on into India. Over several centuries, this wandering group moved across India, conquering and then settling and merging with the earlier people of the region. Out of this "merger" came a new, highly developed Indian culture and a new religion: Hinduism.

The Hindu Religion. Although Westerners speak of "Hinduism" as though it were one religion, there are in fact many different sects, or branches of this religion. Each sect has its own customs and beliefs. Just as Christianity includes the Catholic Church, the Eastern Orthodox Church, the Russian Orthodox Church, and many different Protestant religions, so does Hinduism include many different beliefs and practices.

Originally, as we have seen, Hinduism grew out of the combination of the original religion of the Indian people and the new religion of the Aryan invaders. The foundation of Hinduism rests on the caste system: the idea that human beings are born into different castes, or categories, each of which serves heaven in its own way. Thus, a person could be born into a caste of a soldier or a merchant or a priest, etc.

Another major part of Hinduism is belief in the Veda, ancient holy writings. Like the Jewish and Christian Bibles and the Moslem Koran, the Hindu Veda talks about the nature of God and the practices that are needed to act in a religious way.

Like other Eastern religions, Hinduism includes reincarnation, the idea that the soul is reborn into a new body after the old body has died. According to Hinduism, how you behave in one life affects the body and the caste that you are born into in the next life. Through one's own actions, especially through the spiritual practices of yoga, it is possible for people to liberate themselves from the cycle of rebirth and human suffering and achieve union with God.

The Birth of the Grand Road. The early Hindu culture—that of the early Indians and the invading Aryans—first developed India's Grand Road. It was not an easy task. They found a region covered with dense forests, where robbers and wild beasts hid and attacked unwary travelers.

But these early Indians wanted better roads than the ancient tracks and trails through this difficult country. They wanted to visit their neighbors, to trade with them and to travel freely. Their early writings praise the *paqthikrits*, or pathfinders, who made new roads by cutting and burning their way through the forests and jungles.

Once the pathfinders marked the trails, the early Indians went on to improve their Grand Road. The main route was built up so that water and wastes could drain from it. Early road workers also made sure that the road offered a firm base for chariots and ox carts.

Much of the land through which the road traveled was marshy, and sometimes the road crossed shallow rivers. So the early road builders made dikes to keep water off the road, or built causeways—

narrow pathways across muddy or watery areas. At deeper rivers, small ferryboats carried travelers across.

Rest houses were also built along the road, so that travelers would have a place to spend the night, or to buy food. Stones marked the way, and also told travelers the distance they still had to travel to the next major city.

For all these improvements, the condition of the road was uneven. Some places kept the road in good repair; other places allowed it to fall into disrepair. At this time, the area we know as India was not one country with one government. It was a collection of small states, all of which made decisions and acted independently of each other.

Dangers of the Road. The Indian Grand Road was certainly not safe. Even in the best of times, there were robbers and raiders. Travelers often prayed to their special god, Manibadra, to protect them from wolves, and from robbers who might take their goods and throw them into deep pits, or hold some of their party for ransom.

Given the dangers, people seldom traveled alone. Instead, they joined together in caravans under a chosen leader, known as the *sartha vaha*. Often local people were paid to go along, to both guard and guide the caravan. Such local experts offered some protection against robbers—and also helped find water on dry parts of the route. In addition, they advised on local plants, some of which were poisonous. Nevertheless, travelers sometimes ate strange leaves, flowers, or fruits—and had to be treated for sickness by the caravan leaders. No food was to be found along the road, so caravans had to carry with them all supplies, besides carrying as much water as possible.

Changing Times

Persians. In the centuries before the birth of Christ, India and its Grand Road saw many changes. In the sixth century B.C., the Aryans, who had settled in Persia several centuries earlier, moved through the northwest passages into India. The leader of these Persians was known as Darius I.

Darius and his Persians got as far as the Beas, the fourth of the Punjab's five rivers. But instead of going farther on the Grand Road, they went down the Indus River to the sea.

For a time, these Persians ruled this northern part of India. While they ruled, they protected the camel caravans that traveled between Persia and India. But they eventually lost control of their Indian territory after a few decades.

The Founding of Buddhism. Another major event in the sixth century B.C. was the birth of Siddhartha Gautama, who became known as the Buddha. The young Siddhartha, son of a king, was raised by his father in great luxury. But at age 29, he renounced the world and went off in search of spiritual truth. By age 35, he believed he had found a new way, and founded the religion that became known as Buddhism. He became known as the Buddha, a title that means "the enlightened one."

Buddhism teaches that there are four "noble truths": that to live is to suffer; that the reason people suffer is because they want something that they do not have; that it is possible to stop wanting

Prince Siddhartha, better known later as the Buddha, traveled to school in an ox-drawn chariot, common on the Indian Grand Road. (**Vic**toria and Albert Museum)

things, and thus to stop suffering, a state known as *nirvana*; and that it is possible to reach nirvana by living according to certain principles.

Like Hinduism, Buddhism became a great world religion. Eventually, it spread throughout India, Tibet, Ceylon (modern-day Sri Lanka), China, Japan, and Korea.

Buddha himself wandered all over India, often on the Indian Grand Road, in search of the holy truth. Tales of his passing through were told for centuries after. As Buddha's influence grew, he often found that local kings would ask him to delay his journey until they had time to repair the route. That was often done for important travelers.

Alexander and the Greeks. During the time of Buddha's travels, the region we call India merged into four separate kingdoms from an original number of 16. In the mid-fourth century B.C. came another group of invaders—the Greeks, under the leadership of Alexander the Great.

Alexander was drawn to India by tales of fabulous riches, and of strange animals like elephants, apes, and peacocks.

Alexander fought hard battles with the mountain peoples, eventually overpowering them. Then he crossed the Indus River fairly easily, on a bridge of boats built for him by a local king.

After this point, though, it became hard for Alexander to move his army farther into India. At the Beas River, the Greek soldiers refused to go on. Alexander was forced to turn back toward home.

Alexander died not long after. Although his stay in India had been brief, his influence was lasting. His heirs set up kingdoms in nearby Central Asia. And they brought Greek art to India, including Greek coins with Alexander's head stamped on them. Greek art strongly shaped the Buddhist art that was later adopted from India throughout much of Asia.

THE MAURYANS

A New Dynasty. Northern India was to see an even more lasting change, with the rise of a great Indian leader. While Alexander was working his way toward the Indus, Chandragupta Maurya was working to unite the area along India's Grand Road.

Chandragupta took the throne of the state of Magadha, which was centered in the Ganges basin. He also took control of the eastern part of the Grand Road. The Mauryan heirs expanded their control and influence even farther. By the time of the great king Asoka in 250 B.C., the whole of the Grand Road was theirs.

Keeping the Road in Good Repair. The Mauryans made the Grand Road safer and kept it in a better state of repair than ever before. They created a state official whose job it was to keep the highway open and in good repair. Under this official, causeways and ferries were built and maintained; milestones and signposts were put up all along the route, and wells were dug where needed, so that travelers could find water on the way.

This country scene from the first century B.C. includes a four-horse chariot that could only have been used on good roads. (From a terracotta plaque found near Allahabad)

In addition, trees were cut down where they blocked the road, or planted beside the road where they might provide shade. A special labor force seems to have worked on the road, removing stones that blocked traffic. Armies and sometimes large caravans also carried groups that made repairs or put up needed shelters. Guardhouses were also put up for government messengers.

In the northern, dry parts of the Indian Grand Road, travelers often rode camels, the "ships of the desert." (By Henry Ainslie, 1852, India Office Library)

New Trade. At this time, the route itself was 2,600 miles long, but special care was also extended on the route's main branches. By the time of Asoka, these extended far south, down toward the tip of India, toward the port cities of Barygaza (also known as Bharukachchcha, or Broad) and Barbaricon. These ports were major cities on the Spice Route, the trade for spices, silks, jewels, porcelain, and other goods between China, India, and the lands of the Far East.

Now trade and travel flourished in India, and nowhere more than on the Grand Road. Merchants had always traded on the route. At first they used a simple barter system for cloth, leather, and animals. By Mauryan times, money was still not used much in this part of the world. Greek and Roman coins were rare and were highly prized. But traders sometimes carried their own scales and weighed out gold in exchange for goods.

During Mauryan times, the range of goods passing through India expanded greatly. Furs and the highly prized horses of Central Asia came into India by way of the northwest passes. Woven and embroidered shawls came from the mountains of Kashmir and Nepal and from the Punjab. There were also linens, silks, and cottons from the major cities of the Ganges Basin, and from China. Precious stones and pearls came from India, Ceylon, Persia, Burma, and other places along the Spice Route. Fragrant woods and incense, such as sandalwood, came from Southeast Asia.

Pilgrims, like these shown in a Mathura stone mural, were frequent travelers on the Indian Grand Road. (State Museum, Lucknow, second century)

Some of the caravans on the Indian Grand Road were huge. They included elephants, horses, oxen, donkeys, camels, buffaloes, chariots, carts, litters, palanquins (covered chairs for the rich, carried on the shoulders of four or more men), merchants carrying packs on their backs, and walkers. One poet called the caravans "a moving ocean of men."

Often pilgrims, or religious travelers, were on the road, seeking to visit the holy places of Buddhism. Some tried to follow Buddha's exact footsteps on his journey in search of enlightenment. Buddhism became especially widespread after the Mauryan King Asoka converted in the mid-third century B.C. Buddhist pilgrims often traveled with peddlers or became caravan leaders themselves.

Jainism: A New Religion. Jainism was founded in the sixth century B.C., partly in protest against the rituals of Hinduism. Jainism was founded by 24 saints, the last of whom was named Vardhamana, but who was called Mahavira or Jina. The name "Jainism" comes from the name "Jina." Jina preached the need for an ascetic life—that is, a life removed from the pleasures of the world. He also preached the need for concern for all life. He and his followers believed that these two principles would help them escape the cycle of always being reincarnated and allow them to reach nirvana, the union with God.

The Jain religion was popular among merchants and traders. It also motivated many travelers along India's Grand Road to visit Jain shrines and to preach their religion.

Jainists had to avoid travel during the four rainy months of the year—June through September. They had to avoid dangerous routes, where forests sheltered robbers, or where there was no government. And they had to follow strict dietary rules, begging for their food on the way. Most Indian pilgrims followed this last practice, for it was believed that to beg from someone was a kindness: it allowed that person to practice a charitable act.

Life with a Caravan. Along with the caravans often went traveling performers. Actors, dancers, jugglers, and acrobats often went from town to town, performing for a few coins and then moving on. In addition, laborers looking for work were often on the road. So were students and young people traveling to complete their educations.

To make it easy for all travelers, caravans were supposed to move slowly enough for old men and children to keep up. They were also supposed to stop for midday meals. They followed the main route, where beggars—including most pilgrims—could ask for alms (gifts or handouts), and where the animals could find proper grazing.

Caravans sometimes faced dangers like robbers, floods, wild elephants, or tigers. Then they might camp along the road to wait out the danger and to form a united front with other caravans. Travelers would often form a circle of wagons for defense. Most caravans carried fencing or thorny bushes that could be placed around the camp to ward off wild animals.

Passports and Tax Collectors. Whatever the type of traveler, all were highly regulated in Mauryan times. Passports were needed by all Indians or foreigners who traveled in the countryside. These were checked by the "superintendent of meadows," who ran inspection houses at key points along the main roads.

These superintendents ran the shelters and wells that lined the roads. They used dogs and hunters to find robbers or dangerous animals that might threaten the caravans. They warned travelers of danger by shouting and clanging bells or pans.

Tax collectors also worked along the main roads. There were customshouses at the main gateways of each city. Customshouses were places where travelers had to pay tariffs, or taxes, on the value of the goods they were bringing in or out of a city.

Once through customs, merchants could set out their goods for sale. But they had to stay in the shadow of the customshouse flag, for the state controlled prices. A director of trade fixed prices throughout the country. Sometimes he himself bought and sold goods—and set prices for them so as to enrich his king!

Other superintendents ran the ports and the ferry crossings. They set the ferryer's prices. However, they did not ensure that the ferryer would be paid. For centuries, people who ran the ferries were told to collect their fares before crossing. Otherwise, they might not get them.

The Decline of the Mauryans. This well-organized system along the Indian Grand Road fell apart after the death of Asoka. Then the Mauryan Empire broke into two dozen smaller states.

The next few centuries saw a series of invasions through the northwest passes. These invasions were all part of the major changes taking place among the nomadic peoples of Central Asia. The first was the invasion of Indo-Greeks from the land of Bactria (modern Afghanistan). These were the heirs of Alexander the Great. In about 175 B.C., these Indo-Greeks moved down the Grand Road to take control of northern India from the Indus to the Ganges.

The Indo-Greeks only held power for about 10 years. But many Indo-Greeks stayed behind, and their influence was felt for at least another century.

A few decades later, a Central Asian people called the Sakas moved deep into India but were eventually defeated and driven out.

THE KUSHANS

Next came the Kushans, warlike people from southern Russia. They invaded India from the north, by the lightly defended route over the rugged mountains of the eastern Hindu Kush (from which the Kushans got their name). In the decades just before and just after the birth of Christ, they took Taxila and moved into India along the Grand Road.

The Kushans reached as far as the city then called Varanasi (today it's called Benares). Under the Kushans, India became part of a vast empire that extended from the Persian Gulf north to the Jaxartes (Syr) River and east along the Silk Road to Hotan (Khotan), which is now part of China. In fact, the Kushans even pushed back the powerful Chinese Empire. For the first time, the entire route between the Ganges River and Central Asia belonged to one power.

The Kushans kept their main base deep in Central Asia. Their new local capital was at Peshawar, from words that meant "frontier town." (Today, Peshawar is part of the country of Pakistan.) Under them, the Khyber Pass became the main northwest pass into India.

The Kushan Empire didn't bring much that was new to India, but it rather built on the remains of the Mauryan Empire. Through the Grand Road at this time, India exported its culture to the rest of Central Asia. The greatest Kushan leader, Kanishka, was a strong believer in the Indian religion of Buddhism, and he spread that religion throughout the Himalayas and into Central Asia. From there it gradually passed along the old Silk Road, which is how it reached China (and from there, Korea and Japan). Although the Kushans are almost forgotten today, their role in spreading Buddhism throughout Asia was very important.

The Roman and Chinese Empires. While the Kushans ruled in India, the Roman and Chinese empires were at their height. In the first few centuries A.D., these two powerful empires affected the Kushans by their eagerness to trade. Both Eastern and Western Roman empires were happy to trade with India, either by sea, along the Spice Route, or by land, over the Silk Road and the Indian Grand Road.

Of course, the Kushans did not control all of northern India with equal power. In Bengal, along the eastern section of the Grand Road, there was war and unrest. This drove many people, especially traders, to move to Southeast Asia, where they hoped to gain in the spice trade. Even today, there are Indian merchant communities in Southeast Asia.

Along the Indian Grand Road, trade continued and increased. The Chinese traded with the Indians directly; the Romans did so by middlemen, such as Armenians, Syrians, Jews, Greeks, and a people known as the Parthians. Roman trade was very important to India, which wanted Roman grain in exchange for Indian luxuries. Kanishka even adopted Roman coins as the standard currency. The Romans, on the other hand, tried to limit the amount of money they spent in India.

BUDDHIST PILGRIMS

The New Empire of the Guptas. The Kushans ruled India until the fourth century A.D. When their hold weakened, they were replaced by a dynasty of Indian kings called the Guptas. In Gupta times, the whole Grand Road was in use once again, in a united northern India.

Pilgrims Seek Religious Truth. Also on the Gupta routes came many Chinese Buddhist pilgrims. These were Chinese who had been converted to Buddhism and were traveling to India, home of the Buddha. They sought religious truth, and also copies of Buddhist writings that they could not get in China. Many were warmly greeted by Buddhist communities in India, and many stayed in India for several years.

Some pilgrims followed the main route into India. Many others wandered among the Buddhist shrines in the higher mountains, as Buddha himself had done. Imagine how difficult it must have been to form a community in the gigantic Himalayan mountains. Here is a description from one Chinese visitor—Fa-Hsien—although perhaps his description is not quite realistic.

> On these mountains there is snow in winter and summer alike. There are also venomous dragons, which, if provoked, spit forth poisonous winds, rain, snow, sand, and stones. Of those who encounter these dangers not one in ten thousand escapes....[We took] a difficult, precipitous [steep], and dangerous road, the side of the mountain being like a stone wall ten thousand feet in height. On nearing the edge, the eye becomes confused; and wishing to advance, the foot finds no resting place. Below there is a river, named Indus....

The plains of northern India were easier. The people there were used to pilgrims and greeted them warmly. Fa-Hsien describes the usual welcome:

> When traveling priests arrive, the old resident priests go out to welcome them and carry for them their clothes and alms-bowls, giving them water for washing and oil for anointing their feet, as well as the liquid food allowed out of hours.

Hard Times

Religious Changes. Even while Buddhist pilgrims were coming to India from many parts of Asia, Buddhism was declining in India itself. The older Hindu religion was becoming more popular. Buddhist and Jain pilgrims on India's Grand Road were now often joined by Hindu pilgrims traveling to bathe themselves in the holy water of the Ganges River. This trend increased over the centuries as the Guptas weakened and India once again broke apart into many states.

New Invaders: The Huns. In the middle of the sixth century, another group of invaders pushed through the northwest frontier into India. These were the Hunas, part of a Central Asian nomadic people. In the West, they were known as the White Huns. Like early invaders, the Huns moved from Bactria down the Grand Road to the Ganges plain. They cruelly persecuted Buddhists throughout the area now under their control.

Not all of India fell to the Huns. Northeast India—the ancient core kingdom of Magadha, and Bengal to its east—stayed in Gupta hands. But war made the country weak. Even after the Hunas were driven back into the high mountains, the Guptas were powerless.

With the Guptas in a weakened condition, the formerly unified northern India broke apart still further. Visiting pilgrims were saddened by the state of the country, and of the Buddhist religion. Hsüan-Tsang was a famous Chinese pilgrim who visited India in

Hsüan-Tsang was just one of many pilgrims who crossed Asia and circled the Himalayas onto the Indian Grand Road. (From *Toyo Bijutsu Taikan,* c. 800 A.D., Tokyo, British Museum)

the middle of the seventh century. He told a tale of many changes. About one former monastery, he wrote, "Here again silence and desolation reigned where once nearly 20,000 monks studied and meditated and wrote."

Without central control, there was no single power to maintain the roads, which fell into disrepair. The Indian Grand Road suffered. It fell into disrepair and was plagued by robbers.

India itself was no longer a unified nation, but only a group of small states. The Roman Empire had fallen, so that great trading market was gone. Central Asia had been carved into many small states, so they no longer made good trading partners. In those times, little long-distance trade was conducted along India's Grand Road.

ISLAM

In the seventh and early eighth centuries, there came a new force that would change the face of India once again. The religion of Islam, founded in Arabia by the prophet Elijah Mohammed, began to spread throughout Asia, the Middle East, and Africa. By 711 A.D., this new religion extended as far west as Spain, and as far east as China's border in Central Asia.

The History of Islam. Islam was a religion that grew out of Christianity and Judaism. The followers of Islam (called Moslems) believe in the holiness of Adam, Abraham, Noah, Moses, and Jesus, but they believe that God's latest and greatest prophet was Elijah Mohammed. Their holy book is the Koran, written by Mohammed, and their holy city is Mecca, in Saudi Arabia, where Mohammed had lived and developed this new religion.

Islam spread quickly, from Arabia throughout the Middle East, and beyond. Like Christianity, it attracted many passionate followers. And, like the Christians, some of them insisted on converting others to their religion by force. When Moslems conquered a territory, they would demand that the people living there adopt Islam as their new religion.

Islam in India. At first, India resisted this new religion. The northwest passes were well guarded. The lower Indus region was taken by Islamic forces in 712, but the rest of India kept the Moslems out for almost 300 years.

Finally, the Afghan people (ancestors of those who live in the modern country of Afghanistan) converted to Islam. The Afghans controlled and guarded the northwest passes, and so after their conversion, it was easy for the Moslems to invade India.

The Moslems Attack. The Hindu kingdoms along the Grand Road were still fighting among themselves and were not able to meet a threat from the northwest. In 991 A.D., the Moslem Sultan (ruler) Mahmud occupied Peshawar and used it as a base for taking the Punjab. From there, he took and laid waste the great Hindu cities, among them Kanauj, Lahore, and Mathur (these cities are now part of the modern-day Moslem country, Pakistan).

Eventually, Mahmud retired to the Punjab. Then Moslems and Hindus now shared the Grand Road. But the road was more or less neglected, and the peace between Hindus and Moslems was an uneasy one.

The Grand Road Revives. In 1191 the Moslem leader Mohammed Ghori moved east against the Hindu kings. He gained control of the Ganges Valley and made the small town of Delhi his capital. From there, the sultans ruled for the next three centuries. Their empire went down into the Deccan peninsula and went so far as to include Bengal.

Under the Moslem sultans, the Grand Road was renovated. The new government wanted safe and secure roads. They were needed for holding the new territory: good roads made it easier for soldiers to move quickly, keeping subject peoples under control and scaring invaders away.

But as time went by, the roads again became important for trade. Western Asian countries increased trade with India. And immigrants came to India from around the Moslem world—Persia, Africa, and Central Asia. Soon many travelers created a constant flow of traffic on the Grand Road and India's other routes: scholars, musicians, acrobats, clowns, beggars, artisans, political refugees, pilgrims, and just plain adventurers.

There were also many merchants. The Hindus looked down on merchants, for they were said to be of a lower caste. But the Moslems admired merchants. Their prophet Mohammed had praised merchants as "the couriers of the world and the trusty servants of God upon earth."

Making the Roads Safe. The sultans took strong measures to protect the roads. They formed road crews of both hired and forced labor and had them cut down jungles and clear the forests near the roads. That made it more difficult for robbers to hide out. Robbers' dens were emptied and replaced by government forts.

The sultans also converted the *dacoits*—semipermanent robber bands—into the paid protectors of the roads. Indian writer Amir Khusrau described it like this:

> ...the very thieves who, before this, set villages on fire, now lit the lamps and guarded the highways; if a traveler lost a piece of thread, the people of the vicinity either found it or paid its price.

Ziau'ddin Abarani added this:

> ...the highwaymen, inspired by the fear of his [the sultan's] sword, acted as sentinels and protectors of roads. Those who were confirmed and hereditary highwaymen now broke their weapons, sold their bows and shields, and took to ploughing and agriculture.

These moves helped the sultans hold back possible rebellions. They were also able to fight off most of the raids that were still made by the Central Asian peoples to the north.

The result was a revival in travel and trade along the Grand Road. Travel was easier than ever before, with the sultans providing rest houses, wells, shade trees, and signposts along the road. In fact, they went even further, providing reservoirs, canals, and ponds so that people and animals would have enough water for their journey. This process also encouraged the spread of people and farming along the road. Some people said that walking along the Indian Grand Road was now like "walking through a garden."

Even more attractive were the changes made in the rest houses themselves, which the Moslems called *sarais* or *caravansarais*. Shops sold whatever items a traveler might need. They also provided places to stay, food, and water. That meant that travelers no longer had to carry tents and supplies. They could even get fresh horses at the caravansarais.

The Grand Road had official uses as well as economic ones. The sultans used courier relays to send messages quickly. That is, a courier would begin carrying a message then pass it on to another courier stationed farther along the route, who would pass on the message in the same way to another courier. That way, couriers could travel at top speed, with a new courier taking the message as soon as the old one was tired. Courier stations were about one-third of a mile apart for foot courier and four miles apart for horse couriers, so you can see that these messengers were really expected to dash at top speed for these short distances.

The foot-courier carried the message or the package (sometimes special fruits for the sultan) in one hand, and a rod with bells on it in the other. As the sound of bells was heard at the next station, the new courier prepared to run. He took to message and the bells and went on to the next station. This system meant that news could reach Delhi from anywhere in the empire in a maximum of only three days.

THE MUGHALS

In the 14th century, Moslem rule weakened, and some Hindu states revived. Before they could change the balance of power too much, however, new invaders arrived once again from the northwest. In 1398 the Mongols arrived—a people from the area that today is known as Mongolia. Their leader's name was Timur, "the lame," also called Tamerlane.

The Mongols pushed halfway down the Grand Road, almost without a fight. They even took and sacked the imperial city of Delhi. Then they withdrew to Central Asia.

But it was too late for the Moslem regime—its weakness had been made clear. The Moslems' hold loosened and other states along the Grand Road reasserted their independence.

The Second Wave of Mongols. The Mongols returned in the 16th century, and this time they proved to be a more lasting force. They came under the leadership of Babur, or Babar, a descendant of both Tamerlane and the famous Mongol leader Genghis Khan. Babur was a Moslem, but was nevertheless ready to conquer Moslem territories.

The Afghan people were fighting among themselves, which made it easy for Babur to seize their capital, Kabul, in 1503. He used this as his base for attacking India, and he conquered Delhi in 1526.

For a warrior king, Babur had some unusual characteristics. He wrote poetry and loved gardens—influences from the Persians. He always longed to return to his homeland in Central Asia—but, instead, he started a new dynasty in India. Babur's dynasty was called the Mughal or Moghul dynasty, Indian versions of the word "Mongol."

By the time Babur died, his empire had become weak. His son, Humayan, had to retreat to Persia for 15 years. Babur's dynasty seemed to be at an end, for a new Afghan leader arose: Sher Shah.

Sher Shah's Rule. Sher Shah had great governing skills. He reshaped the northern Indian government along Persian lines. He was the one to lay out the course of the modern Grand Road.

Sher Shah also revived and expanded the rest-house system, which had fallen apart under the Mughals. He even provided separate resting places for Moslems and Hindus, with servants for each. Sometimes there were even small mosques for Moslem travelers. These rest houses also acted as spy stations, so that Sher Shah always knew what was happening everywhere in his kingdom.

But Sher Shah's abilities were not enough. After only five years in power, he died and the government he had built fell apart. The Mughal Humayan was then able to take back control of India.

Akbar's New Empire. The heyday of the Mughal Empire commenced during the reign of Humayan's son, Akbar. The empire was based along the Indian Grand Road. Akbar had recognized the importance of the Grand Road. Many sections were widened, especially the section leading to the Khyber Pass. Regular ferries were once again established at the main river crossings.

Akbar also expanded the string of forts along the Grand Road, especially at the crossing point of Attock. Although these forts were supposed to protect travelers, the Mughals had little success at this.

Travel was quite slow in those days. Most travelers rode in ox carts or in camel-trains. It took about three months to travel from Delhi to Bengal. Travelers who were concerned about either safety or speed usually took riverboats when they could.

Many of Akbar's reforms didn't last. But the huge Mughal building projects that Akbar and his successors initiated did last. The Taj Mahal—a great mausoleum at Agra—and the Mughal forts along the Grand Road are still standing today. The Mughals had also brought a Persian influence into India, which remains to this day.

THE EUROPEANS: CONQUERORS FROM THE SEA

In the history of the Grand Road to date, invasions came from the mountain passes to the north and northwest only. At the very end

Akbar is praying on the banks of the Indus, before heading up the river in 1522. (By Lal and Nand, Moghul artists, Victoria and Albert Museum)

of the 15th century, however, India faced new conquerors. European sailors, looking for trade with the East, reached India by sea.

The Spice Route Trade. For many centuries, Europeans had enjoyed the goods of the East: spices, silks, cottons, porcelains, ornaments, and other fine goods that they could not grow or make themselves. These goods came from India, China, Southeast Asia, and the Far Eastern lands of Sumatra, Malaya, and the Spice Islands.

Until the end of the 15th century, the Europeans depended on Arab traders for these goods. The Arabs would sail to India and other points east, then bring the goods back to the Mediterranean, where Europeans could buy them.

Robbers like these in prison threatened travelers on the Indian Grand Road for centuries. (From Fannie Roper Feudge, *History of India*, 1903)

For many reasons, Europeans became dissatisfied with this arrangement. They wanted to learn the Eastern routes for themselves, so that they, too, could find these precious goods.

The Portuguese and the Spanish, in particular, sent out expeditions to learn more about the Eastern world. The Portuguese sent the explorer Vasco da Gama east. He arrived on India's Malabar Coast in 1498. Once da Gama had discovered how to sail around Africa's Cape of Good Hope and eastward to India, he was quickly followed by Dutch, French, Danish, and British explorers and traders.

The Europeans Expand. European traders began to set up trading centers all along the coasts of India. As the Mughal Empire began to fall apart, these European powers fought with each other for control of India.

At first, they were only competing for trade. But gradually they began to annex territory in the name of their countries. The British, especially, expanded their territory along India's east coast and through the Ganges Valley. After 1690, the port of Calcutta, near the mouth of the Ganges, became the main center for the British in the East, together with their trading company, the British East India Company.

By the turn of the 19th century, the Mughal dynasty was in a state of collapse. Several other groups carried on bloody battles all along the Indian Grand Road, each trying without success to control the region. These included the Afghans, the Marathans of central India, and the Sikhs.

The Sikhs: A New Religion. The Sikhs were followers of a new religion that had been founded at the beginning of the 16th century. Their founder, Nanak, taught that all religions were fundamentally the same. He preached the idea of only one God, and opposed the caste system. Nanak also preached the idea of meditation as the way to religious truth. The Sikhs were strongest in the Punjab region. But as the British became stronger, they gradually put down the Sikhs.

War on the Overland Routes. The Indian communities warred with each other along the land routes. The British, however, wanted to keep the routes open and free from fighting to protect trade. Gradually, they took control of the entire region from Bengal to the Punjab and then farther south, and they eventually made an alliance with the Sikhs.

Traveling wagons like these have always made up much of the slower traffic on the Indian Grand Road. (From Fannie Roper Feudge, *History of India*, 1903)

The British in India. The British brought many changes to India. They set up civil service training schools, and changed Indian laws so that they resembled British laws. Many Indians resented the British for taking over their country. For many years, Indians organized uprisings and anti-British groups, trying to regain their independence.

The British strove to maintain the roads, for both military and trading reasons. Under British Governor-General Dalhousie, they rebuilt the Grand Road. For the first time, the road acquired a "metalled" surface, made up of layers of broken stone, carefully graded so that the coarsest stones were on the bottom and the finest were on the top. Dalhousie also laid out a railway line along the Grand Road's route, with branch lines to other major cities.

THE BRITISH-AFGHAN WARS

Soldiers exposed on the plains of Kabul were always at the mercy of Afghans on the heights. (Lithograph by Day and Haghe, 1842)

Several nations wanted control of India and Central Asia. The British were pushing down through Central Asia toward the all-important crossroads where the Indian Grand Road joined the Silk

Road. Persia was pressing from the southwest. This made the central region of Afghanistan very important.

The British wanted a ruler in Afghanistan who would support their interests. They put a puppet ruler on the throne in Afghanistan's capital city, Kabul. They were able to do this because of their superior military force.

The British knew little about this area or its people. They believed they were secure. At first the British positioned their headquarters in the great fort called the Bala Hissar. But their "puppet" ruler demanded that he should use it as a palace. Thus, the British army, the wives and children who joined them, and the thousands of support staff all moved to an open camp, with no defense to speak of. Then the British stopped paying the local tribes for their support. At that point, the Afghans decided to throw out the British.

The British paid no attention to early adverse warnings. Finally, on January 6, 1842, the whole camp—over 16,000 people, though only 4,500 of these were soldiers—was forced out of Kabul by the aggrieved Afghans. This was in the middle of winter. They knew nothing about the route, and they had not prepared for the journey. There were fierce Afghan fighters on the hillsides all along the way. Imagine making such a journey, especially with young children.

It took seven days for the British to fight their way over the 110 miles from Kabul to Jalalabad, the nearest British fort. On January 13, one single man on a horse from the group arrived at that fort. Sir John Kaye was there, and wrote: "A shudder ran through the garrison. That solitary horseman looked like the messenger of death ...he now reported his belief that he was the sole survivor of some sixteen thousand men."

Of course, not all of them were men. And there were a few other survivors, people who had been taken hostage and released later. But overall, the British presence in Afghanistan had proved to be a disaster.

The British later managed to regain control of Kabul and fought a series of wars with the Afghans. But for the rest of the time they occupied India, they kept their northwest border at the Khyber Pass. They were not able to "conquer" Afghanistan again.

The British and the Grand Road. Perhaps because of their Afghan experience, the British were very concerned with keeping the Grand Road secure. There were rebel attacks and mutinies along the road, especially in the northwest. But overall the British managed to maintain a tight grip on the road and on the nearby railway.

HIMALAYAN EXPLORERS

The great powers of Europe continued to fight for control over Central Asia. Thus the British were up against both European and Asian peoples in their efforts to control the region. Under these circumstances, information became vital. Many British explorers took to the Himalayas, to explore the old mountain routes, and in order to see if they might suffer attack from that direction.

What they found was a series of rough tracks that were too narrow and too hard for carts. In the mountains, there was no food for livestock along the road, and no rest houses for travelers. Caravans had to carry food for people and animals, often burying part of their supplies to prepare for the return trip.

Diana Shipton wrote of this difficult journey in her book, *The Antique Land*: "Never once until we reached the plains were we out of sight of skeletons. The continuous line of bones and bodies acted as a gruesome guide whenever we were uncertain of the route."

Even so, travelers came, both men and women. Some of the mountain tracks were too hard even for pack animals. They could only be crossed by people on foot. The Europeans often hired local people as porters, to carry their supplies. In *Where Three Empires Meet*, E. F. Knight described the trails:

> On the so-called roads which penetrate these ravines one has to scale cliffsides by means of small wooden pegs let into the rocks, or swarm up a tree-trunk leading from one narrow ledge to another twenty feet above it...a fall of hundreds of feet being the consequence of a false step...Every now and again, in order to circumvent [go around] some impassable precipice overhanging the river, the road abruptly ascended six thousand feet or so, to descend again as steeply on the farther side of the obstacle.

Most of these high mountain passes could only be crossed in the summer, even though they were difficult enough even in that season! Travelers crossing mountain rivers had to watch for icebergs breaking off the glaciers above. In *The Marches of Hindustan*, David Fraser described a typical crossing:

In the very first current, with the water up to my pony's belly, a lump of ice struck him square on the hocks [legs]...If I hadn't been frozen to the saddle by the cold I must have fallen off...It was impossible to cross at right angles owing to the depth and force of the water, and because of the ice. We therefore went down with the stream, edging across when opportunity offered, and returning upstream along the intermediate banks. The crossing occupied about an hour and at the end of it I had to take off my boots to see if my feet were alive.

There were some bridges across these mountain streams, but they were also quite dangerous. Sometimes they were just two ropes— one to walk upon, one to hold onto. In *Listening for the Drums*, General Sir Ian Hamilton wrote of one of the bridges:

> A tight-rope dancer would have been quite all right, I suppose, but these ropes were not tight; they were slack [loose] and sometimes my hands went one way and my feet the other. If I were to live to be a hundred, these crossings will come back to me in nightmares.

Crossing a river gorge on a bridge of ropes was one of the most harrowing experiences faced by travelers in the Himalayas. (By W. Simpson, 1860, Victoria and Albert Museum)

Indian Independence. With unsettled times in Afghanistan and Central Asia, the Indian Grand Road lost much of its long-distance travel and trade in the 19th and 20th centuries. It lost even more importance after 1947. In that year, under the leadership of Mahatma Gandhi, India finally won its independence from Britain. At that time, the route became mainly a series of separate sections, each within the boundaries of an Indian province.

Pakistan. Much of the Indus Valley is now held by the Moslem country of Pakistan. Since 1906, the Muslim League (using an alternative spelling for "Moslem") had been demanding a separate nation from the predominantly Hindu India. When India finally won independence in 1947, the country of Pakistan was created, so that Moslems living in the western part of India would have a Moslem country to live in, separate from Hindu India.

At that time, many Moslems left the rest of India to settle in Pakistan, while many Hindus and Sikhs from the western Punjab moved from the new Moslem Pakistan back into the old India.

Today, Pakistan controls the Grand Road (in the present day called the Grand Trunk Road) from the Khyber Pass to Lahore. The route is cut again in the middle Punjab by the Pakistan-India border between Lahore and Amritsar.

Relations between India and Pakistan have always been uneasy. Since the India-Pakistan War in 1965, the Grand Trunk Road border crossing between the two countries has been closed. Travelers who wish to take this route have to make a long, hard detour.

Afghanistan. Afghanistan also controls part of the Grand Trunk Road. Its capital city of Kabul, the Hindu Kush, and the routes west to Herat and southwest to Kandahar are all in the hands of Afghanistan. When Soviet troops moved south into Afghanistan in 1979, some traffic began to pass on the old route between Afghanistan and its northern neighbor, the Soviet Union.

Bangladesh. The mouths of the Ganges, the region of Bengal, and the route east to Burma lie across yet another border. At first this territory was part of eastern Pakistan. But today it is the independent Moslem country of Bangladesh. While Bangladesh was still part of Pakistan, the Awami League demanded its independence. After a bloody uprising and bitter civil war, Bangladesh won its independence in 1971.

India's Grand Trunk Road. The longest portion of the Grand Trunk Road is still controlled by India, from Amritsar through the Indian capital of Delhi on to Calcutta. Much of the Ganges River is also in India.

The mountain routes to India's north were cut after the 1965 war with Pakistan. At the cease-fire ending that war, India was left in control of the Karakorum route to Hotan. There, however, the route stops, for India's relations with neighboring China have not been friendly.

Other alliances have been formed. One of these resulted in the opening of a new long-distance road: the Karakorum Highway, built by Pakistan and China. The Indian Grand Trunk Road, since the building of the Karakorum Highway, serves mainly modest, local purposes.

The road today reflects its less-than-international status. People on foot, camels, oxen, horses, carts, bicycles, and rickshaws (carts drawn by a person peddling a bicycle) all share the road with buses, trucks, and cars. The road in the Punjab generally consists of three broad strips across the countryside. The paved, raised midsection is a double-lane highway for motor traffic. On both sides are dusty lanes for travelers going on foot or with animals.

Walkers, drovers, carters, and truckers still spend the night at rest houses, which are now sometimes called hostels. Monasteries still shelter pilgrims and other travelers who honor their religious customs. There are also many campsites along the Grand Trunk Road, where the land is trampled hard from hundreds or even thousands of years of use. And up in the mountains, a dusty caravan track still runs parallel to the motor highway and rail line through the narrow Khyber Pass.

SUGGESTIONS FOR FURTHER READING

Chandra, Moti. *Trade and Trade Routes in Ancient India* (New Delhi: Abhinav Publications, 1977).

Fairley, Jean. *The Lion River: The Indus* (New York: John Day, 1975).

Grousset, René. *In the Footsteps of the Buddha* (New York: Grossman Publishers, 1971), translated from the French by J. A. Underwood.

Moreland, W. H., and Atul Chandra Chatterjee. *A Short History of India*, 4th edition (New York: McKay, 1967).

Panikkar, K. M. *A Survey of Indian History*, 3rd edition (Bombay: Asia Publishing House, 1962).

Sabir, Mohammad Shafi. *Story of Khyber* (Peshawar: University Book Agency, 1966).

Spear, Percival. *A History of India*, 2 vols. (Baltimore: Penguin, 1965).

Swinson, Arthur. *North-West Frontier: People and Events 1839-1947* (New York: Praeger, 1967).

Verma, H. C. *Medieval Routes to India: Baghdad to Delhi: A Study of Trade and Military Routes* (Calcutta: Naya Prokash, 1978).

Wiles, John. *The Grand Trunk Road: Khyber to Calcutta* (London: Elek, 1972).

INDEX